I0784610

Wallace D. Wattles, Ernest Holmes

The Science of Getting Rich & Creative Mind and Success

OK Publishing 2021

Wallace D. Wattles, Ernest Holmes

The Science of Getting Rich & Creative Mind and Success

Practical Guide to Prosperity and Wealth

Published by

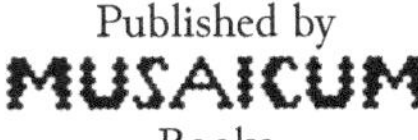

Books

- Advanced Digital Solutions & High- Quality book Formatting -

musaicumbooks@okpublishing.info

2021 OK Publishing

ISBN 978-80-272-7321-8

Contents

Creative Mind and Success

PART ONE - INSTRUCTION

An Inquiry Into The Truth

An inquiry into Truth is an inquiry into the cause of things as the human race sees and experiences them. The starting point of our thought must always begin with our experiences. We all know that life *is,* else we could not even think that we are. Since we can think, say and feel, we must be. We live, we are conscious of life; therefore we must be and life must be. If we are life and consciousness (self-knowing) then it follows that we must have come from life and consciousness. Let us start, then, with this simple fact: *Life is and life is conscious.*

But what is the nature of this life; is it physical, mental, material or spiritual? A little careful thinking based upon logic, more than any merely personal opinion, will do much in clearing up some of these questions that at first seem to stagger us with their bigness.

But what is the nature of this life; is it physical, mental, material or spiritual? A little careful thinking based upon logic, more than any merely personal opinion, will do much in clearing up some of these questions that at first seem to stagger us with their bigness.

The next question is, how do things come from life? How do the things that we see come from the things that we do not see? The things that we see must be real because we see them. To say they are not real will never explain them nor answer any question about them. God's world is not a world of illusion but one of divine realities. The truth must not explain away things that we see. It must explain what they are. We are living and experiencing varying degrees of consciousness and conditions. Only when the why of this living and of our experiences is understood will we know the least thing about the truth, did not say that things are illusions. He said that we must not judge from the standpoint of the seen but must judge righteously or with right judgment; and He meant that we must get behind the appearance and find out what caused it. So let us not in any way fool ourselves nor allow ourselves to believe we have always been fooled. We are living in a world of realities. Whatever we have experienced is a reality as far as that experience is concerned, although if we had had a higher understanding of life, the unpleasant experience might have been avoided.

What Life Is

In the first place, what do we mean by life? We mean that which we see, feel, hear, touch or taste, and the reason for it. We must have come into contact with all we know of life. We have already found what life is or we could not have had any of these experiences. "In the beginning was God" or life. Out of this life which is, everything which is is made. So life must flow through all things. There is no such thing as dead matter. Moreover, life is one, and it cannot be changed except into itself. All forms are forms of this unity and must come and go through some inner activity. This inner activity of life or nature must be some form of self-consciousness or self knowing. In our human understanding we would call this inner knowing, or consciousness, "thought." The Spirit, or Life, or God, must make things out of Himself through self-recognition, or self-knowing or, as we would call it thinking. Since God is all, there is nothing to hinder Him from doing what He wishes, and the question, "How do things come into being?" is answered: God makes them out of Himself. God thinks, or knows, and that thing which He thinks or knows appears from Himself, and is made out of Himself. There is no other possible explanation for what we see. Unless people are willing to begin here, they will never understand how it is that things are not material but spiritual.

Man's Place In Creation

But where does man come in? He is. Therefore it follows that he, too, is made out of God, since God, or Spirit, is all. Being made out of God, he must partake of His nature, for we are "made in His image."

Man is a center of God in God. Whatever God is in the Universal, man must be in the individual world. The difference between God and man is one of degree and not of quality. Man is not self made; he is made out of 'God.

The question might arise, why did God do this? No living person can answer this question. This is something that is known only of the Father. We might suppose that God made man to live with Him and to enjoy with Him, to be one with the Father. It is true, indeed, that those who have felt this most deeply have had a corresponding spiritual power that leads us to suppose that God really did make man as a companion. Man is the individual and God is the Universal. "As the Father hath life within Himself, so hath he given it to the Son to have life within himself." Man's mind is made out of God's mind, and all that man is or ever will be, all that he has or ever will have, must partake of the Divine nature. Man did not make it so, but it is so, and he must accept the fact and see what he can do with it. If he has the same power in his individual life that God has in the Universal, then this discovery will mean freedom from all bondage when he learns how to use his power. As God governs His Universal world so will man govern his individual world, always subject to the greater law and life. This could not be otherwise if we realize what follows from it, for so realizing we find ourselves living in a very different world from the one in which we thought we were living. God governs not through physical law as result, but first by inner knowing-then the physical follows. In the same way, man governs his world by the process which we will call, for want of a better name, the power of his thought.

Man's inner life is one with the Father. There can be no separation, for the self-evident reason that there is nothing to separate him from God, because there is nothing but life. The separation of two things implies putting a different element between them; but as there is nothing different from God, the unity of God and man is firmly established forever. "My Father and I are One" is a simple statement of a great soul who perceived life as it really is and not from the mere standpoint of outer conditions.

Taking as the starting point that man has the same life as God, it follows that he uses the same creative process. Everything is one, comes from the same source and returns again to it. "The things which are seen are not made of the things which do appear." What we see comes from what we do not see. This is the explanation of the whole visible universe, and is the only possible explanation.

As God's thought makes worlds and peoples them with all living things, so does our thought make our world and peoples it with all the experiences we have had. By the activity of our thought things come into our life, and we are limited because we have not known the truth; we have thought that outside things controlled us, when all the time we have had that within which could have changed everything and given us freedom from bondage.

The question, then, naturally arises: Why did God create man and *make him a free agent?* If God had created us in such a way as to compel us to do or to be anything that was not of our choosing, we should not have been individuals at all, we should be automatons. Since we know that we are individuals, we know that God made us thus; and we are just discovering the reason why. Let any man wake up to this, the greatest truth in all ages, and he will find it will answer all questions. He will be satisfied that things are what they are. He will perceive that he may use his own God-given power so to work, to think and to live that he will in no way hinder the greater law from operating *through* him. According to the clearness of his perception and the greatness of his realization of this power will he provide within himself a starting point through which God may operate. There will no longer be a sense of separation, but in its place will come that divine assurance that he is one with God, and thus will he find his freedom from all suffering, whether it be of body, mind or estate.

The Beginning Of Understanding

Man is beginning to realize that he has life within himself as the great gift of God to him. If he really has life, if it is the same nature as the life of God, if he is an individual and has the right of self-choice which constitutes individuality; then it follows that he can do with his life what the wants to do: he can make out of Himself that which he wishes. Freedom is his, but this freedom is within law and never outside it. Man must obey law. If he disobeys it, it has to act as law, and so acting has to punish him. This he cannot change but must submit to. Freedom comes to the individual from understanding the laws of his own life, and conforming to them, thereby subjecting them to his use, to the end of health, happiness and success.

Law obtains throughout all nature, governing all things, both the seen and the unseen. Law is not physical or material but mental and spiritual. Law is God's method of operation. We should think of God as the great Spirit whose sole impulse is love, freely giving of Himself to all who ask and ref using none. God is our Father in every sense of the term, watching over, caring for and loving all alike. While all is love, yet, in order that things may not be chaotic, all is governed by law. And as far as you and I are concerned, this law is always mental.

Our Conditions Governed By Our Thinking

It is easy for the average person to see how it is that mind can control, and to a certain extent govern, the functions of the body. Some can go even further than this and see that the body is governed entirely by consciousness. This they can see without much difficulty, but it is not so easy for them to see how it is that thought governs their conditions and decides whether they are to be successes or failures.

Here we will stop to ask the question: If our conditions are not controlled by thought, by what, then, are they controlled? Some will say that conditions are controlled by circumstances. But what are circumstances? Are they cause or are they effect? Of course they are always effect; everything that we see is an effect. An effect is something that follows a cause, and we are dealing with causation only; effects do not make themselves, but they are held in place by mind, or causation.

If this does not answer your thought, begin over again and realize that behind everything that is seen is the silent cause. In your life you are that cause. There is nothing but mind, and nothing moves except as mind moves it. We have agreed that, while God is love, yet your life is governed absolutely by mind, or law. In our lives of conditions we are the cause, and nothing moves except as our mind moves it.

The activity of our mind is thought., We are always acting because we are always thinking. At all times we are either drawing things to us or we are pushing them away from us. In the ordinary individual this process goes on without his ever knowing it consciously, but ignorance of the law will excuse no one from its effects.

"What," someone will say, "do you think that I thought failure or wanted to fail?" Of course not. You would be foolish to think that; but according to the law which we cannot deny, you must have thought things that would produce failure. Perhaps you thought that failure *might* come, or in some other way you gave it entrance to your mind.

Thinking back over the reason for things, you will find that you are surrounded by a mind, or law, that casts back at the thinker, manifested, everything that he thinks. If this were not true, man would not be an individual. Individuality can mean only the ability to think what we *want* to think. If that thought is to have power in our lives then there has to be something that will manifest it. Some are limited and bound by law through ignorance. This law is sometimes called "Karma," it is the law that binds the ignorant and gives freedom to the wise.

We live in mind; and it can return to us only what we think into it. No matter what we may do, law will always obtain. If we are thinking of ourselves as poor and needy, then mind has no choice but to return what we have thought into it. At first this may be hard to realize, but the truth will reveal to the seeker that law could act in no other way. Whatever we think is the pattern, and mind is the builder. Jesus, realizing this law, said, "It is done unto you even as you have believed." Shall we doubt but that this great Way Shower knew what he was talking about? Did He not say, "It is done unto you"? What a wonderful thought. "It is done unto you." Nothing to worry about. "It is done unto you." With a tremendous grasp of the power of true spiritual thought, Jesus even called forth bread from the ethers of life, and at no time did He ever fail to demonstrate that when one knows the truth he is freed by that knowledge.

Unconscious Creation

The author once attended a patient who was suffering from a large growth. She was operated on and about fifty pounds of water were removed. In a few days the growth had returned. Where did it come from? Not from eating or drinking. Neither did it move from one part of the body to another part, as that would not have increased her weight. It must have been created from elements which she took in from the air. It had to come from something not physically seen, something appearing from nothing that we see. What we call "creation" is the same thing-the visible appearing from the invisible. Was not this phenomenon a creation?

Cases as remarkable as this are occurring every day. We should not deny this fact but try to explain it. In the case of this woman there must have been an activity of thought molded forth into form, else how could this growth have appeared? There is nothing manifest but that there is a cause for the manifestation. Investigation proves that behind every condition, whether of body or environment, there has been some thought, conscious or unconscious, which produced that condition. In the case of this woman the thought was not conscious. But creation is going on all the time; we should realize this and learn how to control it so that there may be created for us the things that we desire and not those that we do not want. Is it any wonder that the Bible says, "With all thy getting get understanding"? Jesus understood all this, and so it was no more effort for Him to do what He did than it is for us to breathe or to digest our food. He *understood,* that is all. Because Jesus did understand and did use these great laws with objective consciousness, people thought He must be God. And when to-day something unusual occurs, people think that a miracle has been performed. Jesus was not God. He was the manifestation of God; and so are all people. "I say that ye are gods, and every one of you sons of the Most High." A thinking person will be compelled to admit, in view of all this, that creation is first spiritual, through mental law, and then physical in its manifestation.

Man does not really create. He uses creative power that already is. Relatively speaking, he is the creative power in his own life; and so far as his thought goes, there is something that goes with it that has the power to bring forth into manifestation the thing thought of. Hitherto men have used this creative power in ignorance and so have brought upon themselves all kinds of conditions, but today hundreds of thousands are beginning to use these great laws of their being in a conscious, constructive way.

Herein lies the great secret of the New Thought movements under their various names and cults and orders. All are using the same law even though some deny to others the real revelation. We should get into an attitude of mind wherein we should recognize the truth wherever we may find it. The trouble with most of us is that unless we see sugar in a sugar bowl we think it must be something else, and so we stick to our petty prejudices instead of looking after principles.

First Steps

The first thing to realize is that since any thought manifests it necessarily follows that all thought does the same, else how should we know that the particular thought we were thinking would be the one that would create? Mind must cast back all or none. Just as the creative power of the soil receives all seeds put into it, and at once begins to work upon them, so mind must receive all thought and at once begin to operate upon it. Thus we find that all thought has some power in our lives and over our conditions. We are making our environments by the creative power of our thought. God has created us thus and we cannot escape it. By conforming our lives and thought to a greater understanding of law we shall be able to bring into our experience just what we wish, letting go of all that we do not want to experience and taking in the things we desire.

Every person is surrounded by a thought atmosphere. This mental atmosphere is the direct result of thought which in its turn becomes the direct reason for the cause of that which comes into our lives. Through this power we are either attracting or repelling. Like attracts like and we attract to us just what we are in mind. It is also true that we become attracted to something that is greater than our previous experience by first embodying the atmosphere of our desire.

Every business, every place, every person, everything has a certain mental atmosphere of its own. This atmosphere decides what is to be drawn to it. For instance, you never saw a successful man who went around with an atmosphere of failure. Successful people think about success. A successful man is filled with that subtle something which permeates everything that he does with an atmosphere of confidence and strength. In the presence of some people we feel as though nothing were too great to undertake; we are uplifted; we are inspired to do great things, to accomplish; we feel strong, steady, sure. What a power we feel in the presence of big souls, strong men, noble women!

Did you ever stop to inquire *why* it is that such persons have this kind of an effect over you while others seem to depress, to drag you down, and in their presence you feel as though life were a load to carry? One type is positive, the other negative. In every physical respect they are just alike, but one has a mental and spiritual power which the other does not have, and without that power the individual can hope to do but little.

Which of these two do we like the better? With which do we want to associate? Certainly not with the one that depresses us; we have enough of that already. But what about the man who inspires us with our own worth? Ah, he is the man we will turn to every time. Before ever we reach him, in our haste to be near, even to hear his voice, do we not feel a strength coming to meet us? Do you think that this man who has such a wonderful power of attraction will ever want for friends? Will he ever have to look up a position? Already so many positions are open to him that he is weighing in his mind which one to take. He does not have to become a success; he already is a success.

Thoughts of failure, limitation or poverty are negative and must be counted out of our lives for all time. Somebody will say, "But what of the poor; what are you going to do with them; are they to be left without help?" No; a thousand times no. The same power is in them that is in all men. They will always be poor until they awake and realize what life is. All the charity on earth has never done away with poverty, and never will; if it could have done so it would have done so; it could not, therefore it has not. It will do a man a thousand times more good to show him how to succeed than it will to tell him he needs charity. We need not listen to all the calamity howlers. Let them howl if it does them any good. God has given us a power and we must use it. We can do more toward saving the world by proving this law than all that charity has ever given it.

Right here, in the manifold world to-day, there is more money and provision than the world can use. Not even a fraction of the wealth of the world is used. Inventors and discoverers are adding to this wealth every day; they are the real people. But in the midst of plenty, surrounded by all the gifts of heaven, man sits and begs for his daily bread. He should be taught to realize that he has brought these conditions upon himself; that instead of blaming God, man or the devil for the circumstances by which he is surrounded, he should learn to seek the truth, to let the dead bury their dead. We should tell every man who will believe what his real nature is; show him how to overcome all limitations; give him courage; show him the way. If he will not believe, if he will not walk in the way, it is not our fault, and having done all we can, we must go our way. We may sympathize with *people* but never with trouble, limitation or misery. If people still insist upon hugging their troubles to themselves, all the charity in the world will not help them.

Remember that God is that silent power behind all things, always ready to spring into expression when we have provided the proper channels, which are receptive and positive faith in the evidence of things not seen with the physical eye but eternal in the heavens.

All is mind, and we must provide a receptive avenue for it as it passes out through us into the outer expression of our affairs. If we allow the world's opinion to control our thinking, then that will be our demonstration. If, on the other hand, we rise superior to the world, we shall do a new thing.

Remember that all people are making demonstrations, only most of them are making the ones they do not desire, but the only ones they can make with their present powers of perception.

How To Attain Strength

Let us see that we use the right attitude of mind in all that we do, filling ourselves with such courage and power of strength that all thought of weakness flees before us. If any thought of weakness should come, ask this question: Is life weak? If life is not weak and if God is not discouraged, then you are not, never were, and never will be. I should like to see the sickly, discouraged thought that could withstand this attitude of mind.

No! Life is strong, and you are strong with the strength of the Infinite; forget all else as you revel in this strength. You are strong and can say I AM. You have been laboring under an illusion; now you are disillusioned. Now you know, and knowing is using the law in a constructive way. "I and my Father are One;" this is strength for the weak, and life for all who believe. We can so fill ourselves with the drawing power of attraction that it will become irresistible. Nothing can hinder things from coming to the man who knows that he is dealing with the same power that creates all from itself, moves all within itself, and yet holds all things in their places. I am one with the Infinite Mind. Let this ring through you many times each day until you rise to that height that, looking, sees.

In order to be sure that we are creating the right kind of a mental atmosphere and so attracting what we want, we must at first watch our thinking, lest we create that which we should not like to see manifest. In other words, *we must think only what we wish to experience.* All is mind, and mind casts back at the thinker that only which he thinks. Nothing ever happens by chance. Law governs all life, and all people come under that law. But that law, so far as we are concerned, we ourselves set in motion, and we do this through the power of our thought. Each person is living in a world of his own making, and he should speak only such words and think only such thoughts as he wishes to see manifested in his life. We must not hear, think, speak, read or listen to limitation of any kind. There is no way under heaven whereby we can think two kinds of thought and get only one result; it is impossible, and the sooner we realize it the sooner we shall arrive. This does not mean that we must be afraid to think lest we create the wrong image, but it does mean that the way most people think can produce nothing but failure; that is why so few succeed.

The person who is to succeed will never let his mind dwell on past mistakes. He will forgive the past in his life and in the lives of other people. If he makes a mistake he will at once forgive it. He will know that so long as he desires any good, there is nowhere in the universe anything that opposes him. God does not damn anyone or anything; man damns everyone and everything.

God does not make things by comparing His power with some other power. God knows that when He speaks it done; and if we partake of the divine nature we must know the same thing in our lives that God knows in His.

> "I am the master of my fate,
> I am the captain of my soul."

What We Will Attract

We will always attract to us, in our lives and conditions, according to our thought. Things are but outer manifestations of inner mental concepts. Thought is not only power; it is also the form of all things. The conditions that we attract will correspond exactly to our mental pictures. It is quite necessary, then, that the successful business man should keep his mind on thoughts of happiness, which produce cheerfulness instead of depression; he should radiate joy, and should be filled with faith, hope and expectancy. These cheerful, hopeful attitudes of mind are indispensable to the one who really wants to do things in life.

Put every negative thought out of your mind once and for all. Declare your freedom. Know that no matter what others may say, think or do, *you are a success,* now, and nothing can hinder you from accomplishing your good.

All the power of the universe is with you; feel it, know it, and then act as though it were true. This mental attitude alone will draw people and things to you.

Begin to blot out, one by one, all false beliefs, all idea that man is limited or poor or miserable. Use that wonderful power of will that God has given to you. Refuse to think of failure or to doubt your own power.

See only what you wish to experience, and look at nothing else. No matter how many times the old thought returns, destroy it by knowing that it has no power over you; look it squarely in the face and tell it to go; it does not belong to you, and you must know-and stick to it-that you are now free.

Rise up in all the faith of one who knows what he is dealing with, and declare that you are one with Infinite Mind. Know that you cannot get away from this One Mind; that wherever you may go, there, right beside you, waiting to be used, is all the power there is in the whole universe. When you realize this you will know that in union with this, the only power, *you* are more than all else, you are more than anything that can ever happen *to you.*

More About The Power Of Attraction

Always remember that Spirit makes things out of itself; it manifests in the visible world by becoming the thing that it wills to become. In the world of the individual the same process takes place. It is given to man to use creative power, but with the using of this power comes the necessity of using it as it is made to be used. If God makes things out of His thought before they come into manifestation, then we must use the same method.

You can attract only that which you first mentally become and feel yourself to be in reality, without any doubting. A steady stream of consciousness going out into creative mind will attract a steady manifestation of conditions; a fluctuating stream of consciousness will attract the corresponding manifestation or condition in your life. We must be consistent in our attitude of mind, never wavering. lames says, "Ask in faith, nothing doubting, for he that doubteth is like a surge of the sea driven by the wind and tossed. For let not that man think that he shall receive anything of the Lord."

We are all immersed in an aura of our own thinking. This aura is the direct result of all that we have ever said, thought or done; it decides what is to take place in our life; it attracts what is like itself and repels what is unlike itself. We are drawn towards those things that we mentally embody. Most of the inner processes of thought have been unconscious; but when we understand the law all that we have to do is to embody consciously what we wish, and think of that only, and then we shall be drawn silently toward it.

We have this law in our hands to do with as we will. We can draw what we want only as we let go of the old order and take up the new; and this we must do to the exclusion of all else. This is no weak man's job but an undertaking for a strong, self-reliant soul; and the end is worth the effort. The person who can hold his thought one-pointed is the one who will obtain the best results.

But this does not imply the necessity of strain or anything of a strenuous nature; on the contrary, strain is just what we must avoid. When we know that there is but one power we shall not struggle, we shall know, and in calmness we shall see only what we know must be the Truth. This means a persistent, firm determination to think what we want to think, regardless of all outer evidence to the contrary. We look not to the seen but to the unseen. The king of Israel understood this when, looking upon the advancing host of the enemy, he said, "We have no might against this great company, but our eyes are upon Thee"-upon the One Power.

How To Attract Friends

The man who has learned to love all people, no matter who they may be, will find plenty of people who will return that love to him. This is not mere sentiment, and it is more than a religious attitude of mind; it is a deep scientific fact, and one to which we should pay attention. The reason is this: As all is mind, and as we attract to us what we first become, until we learn to love we are not sending out love vibrations, and not until we send out love vibrations can we receive love in return.

One of the first things to do is to learn to love everybody. If you have not done this, begin to do so at once. There is always more good than bad in people, and seeing the good tends to bring it forth. Love is the greatest healing and drawing power on earth. It is the very reason for our being, and that explains why it is that people should have something or somebody to love.

The life that has not loved has not lived; it is still dead. Love is the sole impulse for creation; and the man who does not have it as the greatest incentive in his life has never developed the real creative instinct. No one can swing out into the Universal without love, for the whole universe is based upon it.

When we find that we are without friends, the thing to do is at once to send our thought out to the whole world,-send it full of love and affection. Know that this thought will meet the desires of some other person who is wanting the same thing, and in some way the two will be drawn together. Get over thinking that people are queer. That kind of thought will only produce misunderstanding and cause us to lose the friends that we now have. Think of the whole world as your friend; but you must also be the friend of the whole world. In this way and with this simple practice you will draw to you so many friends that the time will be too short to enjoy them all. Refuse to see the negative side of anyone. Refuse to let yourself misunderstand or be misunderstood. no not be morbid. Know that everyone wants you to have the best; affirm this wherever you go and then you will find things just as you wish them to be.

The atmosphere created by a real lover of the race is so powerful that although his other shortcomings may be many, still the world will love him in return. "To him who loveth much, much will be forgiven." People are dying for real human interest, for someone to tell them that they are all right. Which person do we like the better: the one who is always full of trouble and faultfinding, or the one who looks at the world as his friend and loves it? The question does not need to be asked; we know that we want the company of the person who loves and loving, forgets all else.

The only reason we think other people are "queer" is because they do not happen to think as we do. We must get over this little, petty attitude and see things in the large. The person who sees what he wants to see, regardless of what appears, will some day experience in the outer what he has so faithfully seen within.

From selfish motives alone, if from no loftier reason, we cannot afford to find fault or to hate or even to hold in mind anything against any living soul. The God who is love cannot hear the prayer of the man who is not love. Love and co-operation will yet be found to be the greatest business principle on earth. "God is Love."

We will make our unity with all people, with all life. We will affirm that God in us is unified with God in all. This One is now drawing into our life all love and fellowship. I am one with all people, with all things, with all life. As I listen in the silence the voice of all humanity speaks to me and answers the love that I hold out to it.

This great love that I now feel for the world is the love of God, and it is felt by all and returned from all. Nothing comes in between because there is nothing but love to come in between. I understand all people and that understanding is reflected back to me from all people. I help, therefore I am helped. I uplift, therefore I am uplifted. Nothing can mar this perfect picture of myself and my relations with the world; it is the truth, the whole truth, and nothing but the truth. I am now surrounded by all love, all friendship, all companionship, all health, all happiness, all success. I am one with life. I wait in the silence while the Great Spirit bears this message to the whole world.

The Control Of Thought

The man who can control his thought can have and do what he wishes to have and to do; everything is his for the asking. He must remember that whatever he gets is his to use but not his to hold. Creation is always flowing by and we have as much of it as we can take and use; more would cause stagnation. We are relieved of all thought of clinging to anybody or anything. Cannot the Great Principle' of Life create for us faster than we can spend or use? The universe is inexhaustible; it is limitless; it knows no bounds and has no confines. We are not depending on a reed shaken by the wind, but on the *principle of life itself,* for all that we want, have or ever shall have.

It is not *some* power, or *a great* power, we affirm again; it is ALL POWER. All that we have to do is to believe this and act as though it were so, never wavering, not even once, no matter what happens.

As we do this we shall find that things are steadily coming our way, and that they are coming without that awful effort that destroys the peace of the majority of the race. We know that there can be no failure in the Divine Mind, and this Mind is the Power on which we are depending. Now just because we are depending upon Divine Mind we must not think that we do not have to do our share. God will work through us if we will let Him, but we must act in the outer as though we were sure of ourselves. Our part is to believe, and then to act in faith.

Jesus went to the tomb of Lazarus believing and knowing that God was working through Him. Often we may have to go somewhere or do something and we must know with deep conviction that there will be a power going with us that none can gainsay. When we feel this secure place in our thought, all that we will have to do is to act. There is no doubt but that the *creative power of the universe will answer; it always does.* And so we need not take the worry upon ourselves, but rather we will "Make known our requests with thanksgiving."

When Jesus said, "All things whatsoever ye pray and ask for, believe that ye receive them and ye shall have them," he was uttering one of those many deep truths that were so clear to Him and that we are just beginning to see. He knew that everything is made out of mind and that without that positive acceptance on the part of the individual there is no mold into which mind can pour itself forth into form. In the mind of God there is the correct mold, the true knowing, but in the mind of man there is not always this true knowing.

Since God can do *for* us only by doing *through* us, nothing can be done for us unless we are positively receptive, but when we realize the law and how it works, then we will provide that complete inner acceptance. By so doing we permit the Spirit to do the work, to make the gift. The reason we can make our requests known with thanksgiving is because we know from the beginning that we are to receive and therefore we cannot help being thankful. This grateful attitude to the Spirit puts us in very close touch with power and adds much to the reality of the thing that we are dealing with. Without it we can do but little. So let us cultivate all the gratitude that we can. In gratitude we will send our thoughts out into the world, and as it comes back it will come laden with the fruits of the Spirit.

Creating Atmosphere

To the student who has realized that all is mind and that everything is governed by law, there comes another thought: it is that he can create, or have created for him, from his own thinking. He can create such a strong mental atmosphere of success that its power of attraction will be irresistible. He can send his thought throughout the world and have it bring back to him whatever he wants. He can so fill his place of business with the power of success that it will draw from far and near. Thought will always bring back to us what we send out. First we must clear our thought of all unbelief.

This book is written for those who believe; and to those who do believe it will come true in their lives. Without mental clearness on the part of the thinker there can be no real creative work done. As water will reach only its own level, so mind will return to us only what we first believe. We arc always getting what we believe but not always what we want. Our thought has the power to reach, in the outer form of conditions, an exact correspondence to our inner convictions.

By thinking, you set in motion a power that creates. It will be exactly as you think. You throw out into mind an idea, and mind creates it for you and sets it on the path of your life.

Think of it, then, as your greatest friend. It is always with you wherever you may be. It never deserts you. You are never alone. There is no doubt, no fear, no wondering; you *know*. You are going to use the only power that there is in the universe. You are going to use it for a definite purpose. You have already fixed this purpose in your thought; now you are going to speak it forth. You are speaking it for your own good. You desire only the good and you know that only the good can come to you.

You have made your unity with life, and now life is going to help you in your affairs. You are going to establish in your rooms such an atmosphere of success that it will become an irresistible power; it will sweep everything before it as it realizes the greatness and the AllMightiness of the One. You are so sure, that you will not even look to see if it is going to happen; you KNOW.

And now your word, which is one with the Infinite Life, is to be spoken in calm, perfect trust. It is to be taken up, and at once it is to be operated on. Perfect is the pattern and perfect will be the result. You see yourself surrounded by the thing that you desire. More than this, you *are* the thing that you desire.

Your word is now establishing it forever; see this, feel it, know it. You are now encompassed by perfect life, by infinite activity, by all power, by all guidance.

The power of the Spirit is drawing to you all people; it is supplying you with all good; it is filling you with all life, truth and love. Wait in perfect silence while that inner power takes it up. And then you know that it is done unto you. There goes forth from this word the power of the Infinite. "The words which I speak, they are spirit and they are life."

The Power Of Words

Man's word, spoken forth into creative mind, is endowed with power of expression. "By our words we are justified and by our words we are condemned." Our word has the exact amount of power that we put into it. This does not mean power through effort or strain but power through absolute conviction, or faith. It is like a little messenger who knows what he is doing and knows just how to do it. We speak into our words the intelligence which we are, and backed by that greater intelligence of the Universal Mind our word becomes a law unto the thing for which it is spoken. Jesus understood this far better than we do. Indeed, He absolutely believed it, for He said, "Heaven and earth shall pass away but my words shall not pass away till all be fulfilled."

This makes our word inseparable from Absolute Intelligence and Power. Now if any word has power it must follow that all words have power. Some words may have a greater power than others, according to our conviction, but all words have some power. How careful, then, we should be what kind of words we are speaking. All this goes to prove that we really are one with the Infinite Mind, and that our words have the power of life within them; that the word is always with us and never far off. The word is within our own mouth. Every time we speak we are using power.

We are one in mind with the whole universe; we are all eternally united in this mind with real power. It is our own fault if we do not use this truth after we see it.

We should feel ourselves surrounded by this mind, this great pulsating life, this all-seeing and all-knowing reality. When we do feel this near presence, this great power and life, then all we have to do is to speak forth into it, speak with all the positive conviction of the soul that has found its source, and above all else never fear but that it will be done unto us even as we have believed.

What wonderful power, what a newness of life and of power of expression, is waiting for those who really believe. What may the race not attain to when men wake up to the real facts of being? As yet the race has not begun to live, but the time is drawing near. Already thousands are using this great power, and thousands are eagerly watching and waiting for the new day.

Why Belief Is Necessary

Always when we pray we must believe. Our idea of prayer is not so much asking God for things as it is believing that we already have the things that we need. As we have said before, this *already-believing* is necessary because all is mind, and until we have provided that full acceptance we have not made a mold into which mind could pour itself and through which it could manifest. This positive belief is absolutely essential to real creative work; and if we do not at present have it, then we must develop it.

All is law, and cause and effect obtain through all life. Mind is cause, and what we term matter, or the visible, is effect. As water will freeze into the form that it is poured, so mind will solidify only into the forms that our thought takes. Thought is form.

The individual provides the form; he never creates or even manifests,-that is, of himself; there is something that does all this for him. His sole activity is the use of this power.

This power is always at hand ready to be spoken into and at once ready to form the words into visible expression. But the mold that most of us provide is a very poor one, and we change it so quickly that it is more like a motion picture than anything else.

Already we have the power; it is the gift of the Most High in its Finite Expression. But our ignorance of its use has caused us to create the wrong form, which in its turn has caused mind to produce the form which we have thought into it. From this law of cause and effect we may never hope to escape; and while we may think of it as a hard thing, at first, yet, when we understand, we shall see it as absolute justice without which there could be no real self-acting, individual life at all. Because of our divine individuality, even God may have to wait our recognition of Him and His laws.

People in business will do well to remember this and so to form their thought that they will be willing to receive what they send out. No thought of discouragement or disorder should ever be created, but only positive assurance, strong thoughts of success, of Divine activity, the feeling that with God all things are possible, the belief that we are One with that Great Mind. These are the thoughts that make for success.

The realization that we are dealing with one and not with two powers enables us to think with clearness. We are not troubled about competition or opposition or failure because there is nothing but life, and this life is continually giving to us all that we could ask for, wish, or think into it.

We can now see how essential it is that thought should be held one-pointed; that we should think always and only upon what we want, never letting our mind dwell on anything else. In this way the Spirit works through us.

Where So Many Fail

The ordinary individual, sitting down to give a treatment to his business, unconsciously does just the thing that he should have avoided; and then he wonders why he did not get the desired results. Most people simply sit and wish for, or long for, something. They may even have a great desire or hope. They may even go so far as to believe that their desire is going to happen. All this is good as far as it goes, but it does not go far enough. What we must do is to provide that already-having-received attitude. This may seem hard at first but we can easily see that it is necessary; and as it is the only way that mind works, this is what we must do.

Power is, and mind is, and life is; but they have to flow through us in order to express in our lives. We are dealing with law; and nature must be obeyed before it will work for us. Just realize that this law is as natural a law as any other of God's laws, and use it with the same intelligence that you would use the law of electricity; then you will get the desired results. We provide the thought form around which the divine energies play and to which they attract the conditions necessary for the fulfillment of the though.

When we give a treatment this is all that we have to do, but before we can do even this we have to clear our minds of all fear, of every sense of separation from the Divine Mind. Law is; but we must enforce it, or use it, in our own lives. Nothing can happen to us that is not first an accepted belief in our own consciousness. We may not always be aware of what is going on within, but practice will enable us to control our thought more and more so that we shall be able to think what we want to think, regardless of what may seem to be the case.

Each person has within himself the capacity of knowing and making use of the law but it must be consciously developed. This is done by practice, and by willingness to learn and to utilize whatever we know so far as we have gone. The individual who has the most power is the one who has the greatest realization of the Divine Presence, and to whom this means the most as an active principle of his life.

We all need more backbone and less wishbone. There is something which waits only our recognition to spring into being, bringing with it all the power in the universe.

Using The Imagination

Just imagine yourself surrounded by mind, so plastic, so receptive, that it receives the slightest impression of your thought. Whatever you think it takes up and executes for you. Every thought is received and acted upon. Not some but all thoughts. Whatever the pattern we provide, that will be our demonstration. If we cannot get over thinking that we are poor then we will still remain poor. As soon as we become rich in our thought then we will be rich in our expression. These are not mere words, but the deepest truth that has ever come to the human race. Hundreds of thousands of the most intelligent thinkers and the most spiritual people of our day are proving this truth. We are not dealing with illusions but with realities; pay no more attention to the one who ridicules these ideas than you would to the blowing of the wind.

In the center of your own soul choose what you want to become, to accomplish; keep it to yourself. Every clay in the silence of absolute conviction know that it is now done. It is just as much done, as far as you are concerned, as it will be when you experience it in the outer. Imagine yourself to be what you want to be. See only that which you desire, refuse even to think of the other. Stick to it, never doubt. Say many times a day, "I am that thing," realize what this means. It means that the great Universal power of Mind is that, and it cannot fail.

Man's Right Of Choice

Man is created an individual and as such he has the power of choice. Many people seem to think that man should not choose, that since he has asked the Spirit to lead him, he need no longer act, or choose. This is taught by many teachers but is not consistent with our individuality. Unless we had this privilege, this power of choice, we would not be individuals. What we do need to learn is that the Spirit can choose through us. But when this happens it is an act on our part. Even though we say, "I will not choose," we are still choosing; because we are choosing not to choose.

We cannot escape the fact that we are made in such a way that at every step life is a constant choice. What we do need to do is to select what we feel to be right and know that the universe will never deny us anything. We choose and Mind creates. We should endeavor to choose that which will express always a greater life and we must remember that the Spirit is always seeking to express love and beauty through us. If we are attuned to these, and are working in harmony with the great creative power, we need have no doubt about its willingness to work for us.

We must know exactly what it is that we wish and get the perfect mental picture of it. We must believe absolutely that we now have it and never do or say anything that denies it.

Old Age And Opportunity

One of the besetting errors of people is a belief that they are too old to do things. This comes from a lack of understanding what life really is. Life is consciousness and not years. The man or woman who is seventy years old should be better able to demonstrate than the man who is only twenty. He should have evolved a higher thought, and it is thought and not conditions that we are dealing with.

Amelia Barr was fifty-three before she wrote a book. After that she wrote over eighty, all of which had a large circulation. Mary Baker Eddy was sixty before she began her work, and she attended to all of her great activities until she passed from this plane to a higher one. The author of this book once took a man who was over sixty, one who thought his chance for success had gone, and through teaching him these principles in a year's time made him a prosperous business man. He is now doing well and was never before in his life so happy. The last time he was interviewed he said that business was increasing every day and that he had not begun yet. Every day he stands in his store and claims more activity. He speaks the word and realizes increase all the time. If this were not true then life would not be worth the living. What is a few years in eternity? We must get over these false notions about age and competition. In the truth the word competition is never mentioned. The people who think about it have never known the truth.

Life is what we make it from within and never from without. We are just as old as we think we are, no matter what the number of years may have been that we have lived on this planet.

Demonstrating Success In Business

All demonstrations take place within ourselves. Creation is eternally flowing through all things. The law is always working from that inner pattern. We do not struggle with conditions, we use principles which create conditions. What we can mentally encompass we can accomplish, no matter how hard it may seem from the outside.

All external things are but the outer rim of inner thought activity. You can easily prove this for yourself. If you are in business, say, running an ice cream stand or counter, and are not doing good business, look carefully into your own thought and see what you will find. You will find that it is an established belief there that business is not good. You are not feeling a sense of activity. You will not find within your thought any feeling of success. You are not expecting many customers.

Now suppose someone comes along and says to you: "What is the matter? Why are you not doing more business?" This is about what the answer would be: "People don't seem to want what I have to sell." Or perhaps something like this: "I am too old to compete with modern methods." Or even: "Well, times are hard." All this is negative thought.

Now this man to whom you are talking does not believe a word you have said. He knows that causation is in mind and not in matter, and he says: "The whole thing is in your own mind; the trouble with you is that you don't feel that you are a success."

Perhaps you have heard something of this before; if so you will ask him what he means, or perhaps you think he is talking about something peculiar; but we are taking it for granted that you are so anxious to do something to make your business a success that you will be willing to try anything, so you ask him to explain. He begins by telling you all is Mind; nothing moves but Mind moves it and that you are a center in this Mind. You do not understand how this relates in any way to your business, but he goes on to say that your thought decides whether your business shall be a success or a failure. Here you become indignant, and ask if he means to tell you that you want to fail. Of course he knows you do not, and he explains that while you wish success, you are thinking failure, fearing it, and that there is a law that makes your thought, never asking questions but at once sets about its fulfillment. You become interested and ask how this can be; in return you are asked this question: "How did anything come into being?" This sets you to thinking and of course you realize that there was a time when nothing existed but life; so whatever has come into being must have come from that life, for what we see must come from that which we do not see. You have to admit that. Then what you do not see must be the Cause of everything; and you must also admit that; and that Cause works by Law; this you are compelled to admit. Then this Law, being everywhere, must be in you; this is harder for you to see; but after much thought you begin to realize that it is so. Then you, without knowing where your thought processes were leading you, have conceded that you, yourself, are the reason for what happens in your life, be it success or failure.

God couldn't make you any other way and at the same time make you a self-choosing individual. This is plain.

Now what are you going to do about it? This is what you must do. For every time that you have thought failure you are going to replace it with strong radiant thoughts of success. You are going to speak activity into your business. You are going daily to see nothing but activity and to know that it is Law that you are using, Universal Law, and as such your thought is as sure as the thought of God.

Daily you are going to give to the Great Creative Mind exactly what you want to happen. You will see only what you desire and in the silence of your soul you will speak and it will be done unto you. You will come to believe that a great Divine Love flows through you and your affairs. You will be grateful for this Love.

It fills your life. It satisfies your soul. You are a different man. You are so filled with activity and courage that when you meet people they will wonder at your energy. They will begin to wish simply to come in contact with you. They will feel uplifted.

In the course of a few months you will be a success. People will come to you and say: "How do you do it?" The answer will be the same that was given to you a few months ago.

Let the man who is speaking to the public do the same thing. Let him daily see throngs of people coming to hear him. Let him see nothing else. He will experience what he feels, and sees.

Always remember this. *Life is from within outward, and never from without inward.* You are the center of power in your own life.

Be sure and not take on false suggestion. The world is full of calamity howlers; turn from them, every one, no matter how great you think they may be; you haven't the time to waste over anything that is negative. You are a success, and you are giving to the Law, every day, just what you want done. And the Law is always working for you. All fear has gone and you know that there is but One Power in all the Universe. Happy is the man who knows this, the greatest of all Truths.

The whole thing resolves itself into our mental ability to control our thought. The man who can do this, can have what he wants, can do what he wishes, and becomes what he wills. Life, God, the Universe, is his.

Money A Spiritual Idea

Many people seem to think that money must be evil, although I have never as yet seen any who did not want a lot of this evil in their lives.

If all is an expression of life, then *money* is an expression of life, and as such, must be good. Without a certain amount of it in this life, we would have a hard time. But how to get it; that is the race problem. How shall we acquire wealth? Money didn't make itself, and not being self-creative it must be an effect. Behind it must be the Cause that projects it. That cause is never seen; no cause is ever seen. Consciousness is cause and people who have a money consciousness have the outward expression of it. People who have it as a sure reality in their mind, have it as an expression in their pocket. People who don't have this mental likeness don't have money in their pockets.

What we need to do is to acquire a money consciousness. This may seem very material, but the true idea of money is not material-it is spiritual. We need to make our unity with it. We can never do this while we hold it away from us by thinking that we haven't it. Let us change the method and begin to make our unity with supply by daily declaring that all the Power in the Universe is daily bringing to us all that we can use. Feel the presence of supply. Know that it is yours now.

Make yourself feel that you now have, and to you shall be given. Work with yourself until there is nothing in you that doubts. Money can not be kept away from the man who understands that all is Mind, and that Divine Law governs his life.

Daily give thanks for perfect supply. Feel it to be yours, that you have entered into the full possession of it now. Refuse to talk poverty or limitation. Stick to it that you are rich. Get the million dollar consciousness.

There is no other way, and this will react into everything that you do. See money coming to you from every source and from every direction. Know that everything is working for your good.

Realize in your life the presence of an Omnipotent Power. Speak forth into It, and feel that It responds to your approach.

Whenever you see anything or anybody whom you think has more than you, at once affirm that you have the same thing. This doesn't mean that you have what is his, but that you have as much. It means that all you need is yours.

Whenever you think about anything big, at once say, "That means me." In this way you learn to unify yourself, in the Law, with large concepts, and according to the way that Law works, it will tend to produce that thing for you. Never let yourself doubt for even a minute.

Always be positive about yourself. Keep watch over the inner workings of your thought, and the Law will do the rest.

Action

The Universe is teeming with activity. There is motion everywhere. Nothing ever stands still. All activity comes from mind. If we want to be in line with things we must move. This doesn't mean that we must strain or struggle, but we must be willing to do our part by letting the Law work through us.

God can do for us only as we will allow Him to do through us. Intelligence gives us ideas and in our turn we work on them. But our work is no longer done in any sense of doubt or fear, for we know that we are dealing with something that never makes a mistake. We proceed with a calm confidence born of the inner trust in a Power that is Infinite. Behind all of our movements, then, is a great purpose, to let the Law work through us.

The Law of Activity must be complied with; we must be willing to take the way of outer activity. Jesus went to the tomb of Lazarus. We may have to go but there will accompany us something that never fails.

This law of activity we must use in our business. So many business places that we go into have such an atmosphere of inactivity, produce such a drowsy feeling, that we at once lose all interest in what is going on. We don't feel like buying. We leave that place without any apparent reason and go into another. Here we feel that all is life, all is motion, all is activity. We feel confident that this is the place we are looking for. We will buy here; we find just what we want; we are satisfied with our purchase and go away cheerful.

Now to create this activity something more than thought is essential. Not that it does not come first, but the one who has this thought of activity will naturally manifest it in vigorous, energetic movement which helps to produce a spirit of activity in his business and in everything he undertakes. Wherever you see a man who does not move, then you will find one whose thought is inactive; the two always go together.

A man in a store or place of business should always be moving his goods. He should always be doing something. People will see this and getting the thought of activity behind it will want to trade there. We are not attracted to a store that always has the same things on the same shelf. The world likes action, change. Action is Life.

Let a clerk in a store think activity and begin to manifest it, even though he may not be waiting on customers, and in a short time he will be waiting on them. Alertness is the word. Always be alert. *There must be mental alertness before there can be physical activity.*

Act as though things were happening even though they may not appear to be. Keep things moving and soon you will have to avoid the rush. Activity is genius. Half the stores that you go into make you sleepy before you get out, and you feel as though you can't get out fast enough. The other half are alive and those are the ones who are doing the business of the world.

The man who is active in his thought doesn't have to sit by himself to think; he works while he thinks and so complies with the Law which has to work through him. The thought of activity makes him move, and the thought of confidence makes his movements sure, and the thought of Supreme Guidance makes his work intelligent.

We must be careful and not get into ruts; always be doing something new and different, and you will find life becomes a great game in which you are taking the leading part.

Life will never become tiresome to the active mind and body. It is so interesting that we wonder if we will ever get enough of it. Some people get into such lazy mental habits that a new idea cannot find entrance. Great things are done by people who think great thoughts and then go out into the world to make their dreams come true.

If you can't find anything new to do, go home and change the bed around, or the piano; put the cook stove in the parlor and eat on the back step for a time. It will start something moving and changing in you that will never stop. The wide awake person can find so many things to do that he hasn't time even to begin in this life and he knows that Eternity is necessary to carry out the ideals that he already has evolved.

Everything comes from Mind, but Mind acts on itself and we must act on ourselves and on conditions; not as a slave but as a master. Be interested in life, if you want life to be interested in you. Act in Life and Life will act through you. So will you also become one of the great people on earth.

Ideas Of The Infinite

Suppose that we wish to draw from the Universal Mind some definite idea, some guidance, some information, some leading. How are we going to do this? First we must become convinced that we can do it. Where do all the inventions come from? Where does Edison get his information about electricity? Where, if not direct from the Mind of the Universe? Everything that has ever come into the race comes direct from Mind. There is nothing else it could come from.

Every invention is but a discovery of something that already is, although we may not have seen it. Where does the harmony of music come from? Where could it originate except in Mind?

Does not a great musician listen and hear something that we do not hear? His ear is attuned to Harmony and he catches it straight from Life itself and interprets it to the world. We are surrounded by the music of the spheres but few of us ever catch the sound.

We are so filled with trouble that the Divine Melody is never heard. If we could see, if we could hear, if we could understand, if we only realized the presence of the All, what could we not do? When a great thought springs up in the mind of an individual, when a great poem is written, when a great work of art is wrought by some receptive artist, it is simply a sign that the veil is thin between; he has caught a glimpse of reality.

But for most of us Inspiration is not to be depended on, and we must take the slower but none the less sure method of receiving straight from the Infinite. The method is a simple one and very effective. When you want to know a certain thing, or how to begin a certain line of action: First, you must be quiet within yourself. You must not be confused by any outward appearance. Never become disturbed by effects. They didn't make themselves and have no intelligence to contradict you.

Be quiet until you realize the presence of absolute Intelligence all around you, of the Mind that knows. Now get a perfect picture of just what you desire. You cannot get a picture unless you know what it is you want. Put your mind in touch with Universal Mind, saying just what you are waiting for. Ask for it, believe that you are receiving it, and wait. After a few minutes declare that you now know, even though you may not seem to know, yet in the depths of consciousness you have received the impression. Give thanks that you now receive. Do this every day until you get some direction. It is sometimes a good thing to do this just before going to sleep.

Never, after you have done this, deny the knowledge that has been given you. The time will come when some idea will begin to take form. Wait for it and, when it does appear, act upon it with all the conviction of one who is perfectly sure of himself. You have gotten understanding straight from the source of all understanding, knowledge from the source of knowledge. All can do this if they will be persistent. It is a sure direction and guidance and will never fail us. But we must be sure that we are not denying in other moments what we affirm in the moments of Faith. In this way we will make fewer mistakes and in time our lives will be controlled by supreme wisdom and understanding.

Don't Be A Leaner

Never lean on other people. You have strength of your own that is great enough to do all that is necessary. The Almighty has implanted genius within the soul of everyone and what we need to do is to unearth that inner genius and cause it to shine forth. We will never do this while we look to others for guidance. "To thine own self repair, wait thou within the silence dim, and thou shalt find Him there."

All the power and intelligence of the Universe is already within, waiting to be utilized. The Divine Spark must be fanned into a blaze of the living Fire of your own divinity. Self-reliance is the word to dwell on. Listen to your own voice; it will speak in terms that are unmistakable. Trust in your own self more than in all else. All great men have learned to do this. Every person, within his own soul, is in direct communication with the Infinite Understanding. When we depend on other people we are simply taking their light and trying to light our path with it. When we depend on ourselves we are depending on that inner voice that is God, speaking in and through man. "Man is the inlet and the outlet to all there is in God." God has made us and brought us up to where we recognize our own individuality; from now on we will have to let Him express through us. If it were different we should not be individuals. "Behold I stand at the door and wait." This is a statement of the near presence of power; but we, the Individual, must open the door. This door is our thought and we are the guardian of it, and when we do open the door we will find that the Divine Presence is right at hand, waiting, ready and willing to do for us all that we can believe.

We are strong with the strength of the Infinite. We are not weak. We are great and not mean. We are One with the Infinite Mind. When you have a real thing to do, keep it to yourself. Don't talk about it. Just know in your own mind what it is that you want and keep still about it. Often when we think that we will do some big thing we begin to talk about it and the first thing we know all the power seems to be gone. This is what happens. We are all sending out into Mind a constant stream of thought; the clearer it is, the better will it manifest; if it becomes doubtful it will not have so clear a manifestation. If it is confused it will manifest only confusion. All this is according to the Law of Cause and Effect, and we cannot change that Law. Too often, when we tell our friends what we are going to do, they confuse our thought by laughing about it, or by doubting our capacity to do so large a thing. Of course this would not happen if we were always positive, but when we become the least bit negative it will react and we will lose that power of clearness which is absolutely necessary to good creative work. When you want to do a big thing, get the mental pattern, make it perfect, know just what it means, enlarge your thought, keep it to yourself, pass it over to the creative power behind all things, wait and listen, and when the impression comes, follow it with assurance. Don't talk to anyone about it. Never listen to negative talk or pay any attention to it and you will succeed where all others fail.

Causes And Conditions

When we realize that life is not fundamentally physical, but mental and spiritual, it will not be hard for us to see that by a certain mental and spiritual process we can demonstrate what we want.

We are not dealing with conditions but with causes. Causes originate only from the unseen side of life. This is not strange as the same might be said of electricity, or even of life itself. We do not see life, we only see what it does. This we call a condition. Of itself it is simply an effect. We are living in the outer world of effects and in the inner world of causes. These causes we set in motion by our thought, and, through the power inherent within the cause, expresses the thought as a condition. It follows that the cause must be equal to the effect and that the effect always evaluates with the cause held in mind. Everything comes from One Substance, and our thought qualifies that Substance and determines what is to take place in our life.

The whole teaching of the *Bhagavad Gita* is that there is but One and that it becomes to us just what we first believe into it. In other words we manifest the unmanifested. This in no way takes away from the omnipotence of God, but adds to it, for He has created something that is able to do this. God still rules in the Universe, but we are given the power to rule in our lives.

We must realize, then, absolutely that we are dealing with a Substance that we have a right to deal with, and by learning its laws we will be able to subject them to our use, just as Edison does with electricity. Law is but we must use it.

The substance that we deal with, in itself, is never limited, but we often are, because we draw only what we believe.

Because we are limited is no reason why the Universe should have limitation. Our limitation is only our unbelief; life can give us a big thing or a little thing. When it gives us a little thing, it is not limited, any more than life is limited when it makes a grain of sand, because it could just as well have made a planet. But in the great scheme of things all kinds of forms, small and large, are necessary, which, combined, make a complete whole. The power and substance behind everything remain Infinite.

Now this life can become to us only through us, and that becoming is the passing of Spirit into expression in our lives through the form of the thought that we give to it. In itself life is never limited; an ant has just as much life as an elephant though smaller in size. The question is not one of size but one of consciousness.

We are not limited by actual boundaries, but by false ideas about life and by a failure to recognize that we are dealing with the Infinite.

Limitation is an experience of the race, but it is not the fault of God, it is the fault of man's perception. And to prove that this is so, let any man break the bonds of this false sense of life and he at once begins to express less and less limitation. It is a matter of the growth of the inner idea.

People often say when they are told this, "Do you think that I decided to be poor and miserable; do you take me for a fool?" No, you are not a fool, but it is quite possible that you have been fooled, and most of us have been. I know of no one who has escaped being fooled about life; you may not have had thoughts of poverty but at the same time you may have had thoughts that have produced it. Just watch the process of your thinking and see how many times a day you think something that you would not want to happen. This will satisfy you that you need to be watchful, that your thought needs to be controlled.

What we need to do is to reverse the process of our thinking and see to it that we think only positive, constructive thoughts. A calm determination to think just what we want to think regardless of conditions will do much to put us on the highway to a greater realization of life.

Of course we will fall, of course the road is not easy, but we will be growing. Daily we will be giving to the Creative Mind a newer and a greater concept to be worked out into the life around us. Daily we will be overcoming some negative tendency. We must stick to it until we gain the mastery of all our thought and in that day we will rise never to fall again.

We must be good-natured with ourselves, never becoming discouraged or giving up until we overcome. Feel that you are always backed by an Omnipotent power and a kind Father of Love and the way will become easier.

Mental Equivalents

One of the most necessary things to remember is that we cannot demonstrate life beyond our mental ability to embody. We give birth to an idea only from within ourselves. What we are, we put into our thinking. What we are not, we cannot put into it.

If we are to draw from Life what we want, we must first think it forth into Life. It always produces what we think. In order to have success, we must first conceive it in our own thought. This is not because we are creators, but because the flow of Life into manifestation, through us, must take the form we give to it, and if we want a thing we must have within ourselves the mental equivalent before we get it.

This is what Jesus meant when he said that we must believe when we pray. This belief is providing within us that something which knows before it sees what it asks for.

For instance, suppose a man is praying for activity (our idea of prayer is the accepting of a thing before we get it) in his affairs. First, before this activity can come, he must have it within himself; he must come to see activity in everything; there must be something that corresponds to the thing that he wants; he must have a mental equivalent.

We find that we attract to ourselves as much of anything as we embody within. As water will reach only its own level, so our outward conditions will re-produce only our inner realizations.

A man will always draw to him just what he is. But we can learn to provide within the image of what we desire and so in a definite way use the law to get just what we need. If at first we do not have a great realization of activity we will have to work on what we do have, and as our outer conditions come up to meet the inner cause, we will find that it will be much easier to enlarge the inner receptivity for something greater and more worth while. Of one thing we may be assured-we must all start somewhere, and that somewhere is within ourselves. In this within we must make the affirmation, and there, too, we must do the real work of realization.

At the first the way may seem hard, for we are constantly confronted with that which seems to be, and we are not always sure of ourselves nor strong enough to overcome, but we may rest content in the assurance that we are growing. Every day we will be providing a bigger concept of life, and with the inner growth we will have an enlarged power to speak forth into the Creative Mind, with the result that we shall get a fresh impulse and be doing a bigger thing for ourselves. Growth and realization are always from within and never from without.

The old race suggestion of fear and poverty and limitation must be done away with and daily we must clear our thought from all that limits the One from showing forth in our life.

Remember that you are dealing with One power, and not with two. This will make it easier, for you do not have to overcome any condition, because conditions flow from within out, and not from without in.

A man going to a new town will at once begin to attract to him just what he brings in his thought. He should be very careful what he thinks. He should know just what he wants and daily give it over to the Supreme Mind, knowing that It will work for him. Old thoughts must be destroyed, and new must take their places. Every time the old thought comes look it squarely in the face and declare that it has no part in your mind. It has no power over you. You state the law and rely on it to the exclusion of all else. Daily try to see more and to understand more, feel every day that you are being especially looked after. There is no special creation for any individual, but we all specialize the law every time we think into it. For all our thought is taken up and something is always done with it.

A good practice is to sit and realize that you are a center of Divine attraction, that all things are coming to you, that the power within is going out and drawing back all that you will ever need. Don't argue about it, just do it, and when you have finished leave it all to the Law, knowing that it will be done. Declare that all life, all love and power are now in your life. Declare that you are now in the midst of plenty. Stick to it even though you may not as yet see the result. It will work and those who believe the most always get the most. Think of the Law as your friend. always looking out for your interest. Trust completely in it and it will bring your good to you.

One Law And Many Manifestations

People often ask if the Law will not bring harm as well as good. This question would never be asked if people understood what Universal Law really means. Of course it will bring us what we think. All law will do the same thing. The law of electricity will either light our house or burn it down. We decide what we are to do with the Law. Law is always impersonal. There is no likelihood of using the Law for harmful purposes if we always use it for the more complete expression of life.

We must not use it for any purpose that we would not like to experience ourselves. This should answer all questions of that nature. Do I really want the thing I ask for? Am I willing to take for myself what I ask for other people? How can we use the Law for evil if we desire only the good? We cannot and we should not bother about it. We want only the good for ourselves and for the whole world; when we have started causation, at once the Law will set to work carrying out our plans. Never distrust the Law and become afraid lest you misuse it. That is a great mistake, all Law is impersonal and cares not who uses it. It will bring to all just what is already in their thought. No person can long use it in a destructive way, for it will destroy himself if he persists in doing wrong. We have no responsibility for any one except ourselves. Get over all idea that you must save the world; we have all tried and have all failed. We may, by demonstrating in our own lives, prove that the Law really exists as the great power behind all things. This is all that we can do. Everyone must do the same thing for himself. Let the dead bury their dead, and see that you live. In this you are not selfish but are simply proving that law governs your life. All can do the same when they come to believe, and none until they believe.

Transcending Previous Conditions

What if at times we attract something that we do not want? What about all the things that we have already attracted into our lives? Must we still suffer until the last farthing be paid? Are we bound by Karma? Yes, in a certain degree we are bound by what we have done; it is impossible to set law in motion and not have it produce. What we sow we must also reap, of that there is no doubt; but here is something to think about; the Bible also says that if a man repents his "sins are blotted out, and remembered no more forever." Here we have two statements which at first seem not to agree. The first says that we must suffer from what we have done, and the second that under certain conditions we will not have to suffer. What are those conditions? A changed attitude toward the Law. It means that we must stop thinking and acting in the wrong way.

When we do this we are taken out of the old order and established in the new. Someone will say: If that is true what about the law of cause and effect? Is that broken? No, it is this way: The law is not broken, it would still work out if we continued to use it in the wrong way; but when we reverse the cause, that is, think and act in a different way, then we have changed the flow of the Law.

It is still the same Law but we have changed its flow, so that, instead of limiting us and punishing us, it frees and blesses. It is still the law but we have changed our attitude toward it. We might throw a ball at the window, and if nothing stopped it, it would break the glass. Here is law in motion. But if someone catches the ball before it reaches the window, the glass will not be broken. Neither the glass nor the law will be broken. The flow of law will be changed, that is all. So can we, no matter what has happened in the past, so transcend the old experience, that it will no longer have any effect upon us. So if we have attracted something that is not best to keep, we will remember that we do not have to keep it. It was the best that we knew at the time, and so was good as far as it went, but now we know more and can do better.

As law works without variation, so does the law of attraction work the same way. All that we have to do is to drop the undesired thing from our thought, forgive ourselves and start anew. We must never even think of it again. Let go of it once and for all. Our various experiences will teach us more and more to try to mold all of our thoughts and desires, so that they will be in line with the fundamental purpose of the Great Mind, the expression of that which is perfect.

To fear to make conscious use of the Law would be to paralyze all efforts of progress. More and more will we come to see that a great cosmic plan is being worked out, and that all we have to do is to lend ourselves to it, in order that we may attain unto a real degree of life. As we do subject our thought to the greater purposes we are correspondingly blest, because we are working more in line with the Father, who from the beginning knew the end. We should never lose sight of the fact that we are each given the individual right to use the law, and that we cannot escape from using it. Let us, then, go forward with the belief that a greater power is working through us; that all law is a law of good; that we have planted our seed of thought in the Mind of the Absolute; and that we can go our way rejoicing in the Divine privilege of working with the Infinite.

Understanding And Misunderstanding

There are many persons who are constantly unhappy because they seem always to be misunderstood. They find it hard to use the law of attraction in an affirmative way, and they keep on drawing to themselves experiences which they would rather have avoided. The trouble with them is that there is always an undercurrent of thought which either neutralizes or destroys whatever helpful thoughts they have set in motion in their moments of greater strength. Such persons are usually very sensitive, and while this is a quality which is most creative when under control, it is most destructive when uncontrolled, because it is most chaotic. They should first come to know the law and see how it works, and then treat themselves to overcome all sensitiveness. They should realize that everyone in the world is a friend, and prove this by never saying anything unkind to any one or about any one. They must within themselves see all people as perfect beings made in the Divine Image; and, seeing nothing else, they will in time be able to say that this is also the way that all people see them. Holding this as the law of their lives they will destroy all negative thought; and then, with that power which is always in a sensitive person, but which is now under control, they will find that life is theirs to do with as they please, the only requirement being that as they sow so must they also reap. We all know that anything that is unlike good is of short duration, but anything that embodies the good is like God, ever present and Eternal. We free ourselves through the same law under which we first bound ourselves.

The ordinary individual unknowingly does something that destroys any possibility of getting good results in the demonstration of prosperity. He affirms his good and makes his unity with it, and this is right, but he does not stop looking at it in others, which is wrong and is the cause of confusion. We cannot affirm a principle and deny it in the same breath. We must become what we want and we will never be able to do that while we still persist in seeing what we do not want, no matter where we see it. We cannot believe that something is possible for us without also believing the same for every individual.

One of the ways of attainment is, of a necessity, the way of universal love: coming to see all as the true sons of God, one with the Infinite Mind. This is no mere sentiment but the clear statement of a fundamental law and that man who does not obey it, is opposing the very thing that brought him into expression. It is true that through mental means alone he may bring to himself things and he may hold them as long as the will lasts. This is the ordinary way, but we want more than compelling things to appear. What we want is that things should gravitate to us because we are employing the same law that God uses. When we so attain this attitude of mind then that which is brought into manifestation will never be lost, for it will be as eternal as the law of God and cannot be destroyed forever. It is a comfort to know that we do not have to make things happen, but that the law of Divine love is all that we will ever need; it will relieve the overworked brain and the fagged muscle just to be still and know that we are One with the ALL in ALL.

How can we enter in, if at one and the same time we are believing for ourselves and beholding the beam in our brother's eye? Does that not obstruct the view and pervert our own natures? We must see only the good and let nothing else enter into our minds. Universal love to all people and to all things is but returning love to the source of all love, to Him who creates all in love and holds all in divine care. The sun shines on all alike. Shall we separate and divide where God has so carefully united? We are dividing our own things when we do this, and sooner or later the Law of Absolute Justice that weighs out to each one his just measure will balance the account, and then we shall be obliged to suffer for the mistakes we have made. God does not bring this agony on us but we have imposed it on ourselves. If from selfish motives alone, we must love all things and look upon all things as good, made from the substance of the Father.

We can only hope to bring to ourselves that which we draw through the avenue of love. We must watch our thinking and if we have aught against any soul, get rid of it as soon as possible. This is the only safe and sure way. Did not Jesus at the supreme moment of sacrifice ask that the Father forgive all the wrong that was being clone to Him? Shall we suppose that 'we can do it in a better way? If we do not at the present time love all people, then we must learn how to do it, and the way will become easier, when all condemnation is gone forever and we behold only good. God is good and God is Love; more than this we cannot ask nor conceive.

Another thing that we must eliminate is talking about limitation; we must not even think of it or read about it, or have any connection with it in any of our thinking, for we get only that which we think, no more and no less. This will be a hard thing to do. But if we remember that we are working out the science of being, though it may seem long and hard at times we sooner or later do it, and once done it is done forever. Every step in advance is an Eternal step, and will never have to be taken again. We are not building for a day or a year, but we are building for all time and for Eternity. So we will build the more stately mansion under the Supreme wisdom and the unfailing guidance of the Spirit, and we will do unto all, even as we would have them do unto us; there is no other way. The wise will listen, look and learn, then follow what they know to be the only way that is in line with the Divine will and purposes. So shall all see that God is good and in him is no evil.

No Unusual Experience

In demonstrating the truth of supply we do not have to experience any peculiar emotion or psychic experience. We do not have to feel any thrills or anything of that sort. While it is true that some of these things may come, yet we should remember that what we are doing is dealing with law, and that as law it will obey us, when we comply with its nature and contact it in the right way. What we are doing, is stating something into Mind, and if the impression is clear in our own minds *that it is* and *that it is done* we have put all the activity we can put into it, until such a time as something happens in the external for us to work upon. So many people say, "I do wish that I could feel something, when I give a treatment." All this is a mistake and is an attempt to give a physical reason for life. What we do need to feel is that, since God is all and is good, he wants us to have only the good; and feeling this we should take what is already made for us. Our attitude towards such a good Father should constantly be one of thanksgiving.

When we begin to prove the power of the truth we will always maintain this attitude. Know that you are dealing with a sure thing and that all you have to do is to know positively into it and wait for the results to come in the outer. Then do what your own good sense tells you to do, for this is the thought of God through you. More and more you will find that you are being led out of difficulty into that freedom which is the Divine birthright of every living soul. Go ahead, then, looking only at the things desired and never at the things not wanted. Victory will always be on the side that the majority of your thoughts rest on in absolute acceptance.

Visualizing

Some people visualize everything that they think of and many think that it is impossible to make a demonstration unless they possess the power to visualize. This is not the case. While a certain amount of vision is necessary, on the other hand it must be remembered that we are dealing with a power that is like the soil of the ground, which will produce the plant when we plant seed. It does not matter if we have never before seen a plant like the one that is to be made for us. Our thought is the seed and mind is the soil. We are always planting and harvesting. All that we need to do is to plant only that which we want to harvest. This is not difficult to understand. We cannot think poverty and at the same time demonstrate plenty. If a person wants to visualize let him do so, and if he sees himself in full possession of his desire and knows that he is receiving, he will make his demonstration. If, on the other hand, he does not visualize, then let him simply state what he wants and absolutely believe that he has it and the result will always be the same.

Remember that you are always dealing with law and that this is the only way that anything could come into existence. Don't argue over it. That means that you have not as yet become convinced of the truth or you would not argue. Be convinced and rest in peace.

Where Demonstration Takes Place

Does demonstration take place in the patient, the practitioner or in the mind of God? Let us see; We are in the mind of God and so it must take place there. But the patient is also in the mind of God or there would be two minds, and so it must take place in the mind of the patient, also. But that is the mind of God, so what does it matter where it takes place? We do not have to project our thought, because Mind is right at hand and never leaves us at any time. All that we have to do is to know within ourselves, and, when we are absolutely convinced, we will have made the demonstration.

As far as the practitioner is concerned, all that he has to do is to convince himself. Here his work begins and ends. There is a power that will look after the rest. Is this not the supreme attitude of faith in higher power? Of course it is, and the more of that faith that we have, the easier it will be for us and the quicker we will receive an answer to our prayer. If you have a simple, childlike faith it will produce; but it should give us a greater faith when we know something of the way that the law operates. It follows, then, that we should, by understanding, have so great a faith that we shall never fail to get the affirmative answer to all of our thoughts. Each victory will strengthen us until the time will come when we will no longer have to say *I hope* or *believe,* but *I know.*

PART TWO - PRACTICE

Treatments

The way to give a treatment is first of all to absolutely believe that you can; believe that your word goes forth into a real creative power, which at once takes it up, and begins to operate upon it; feel that to this power all things are possible. It knows nothing but its own power to do that which it wishes to do. It receives the impress of your thought and acts upon it.

It is never safe to treat for anything that you do not wish to happen. This means that what you would want for another, you must first be willing to receive for yourself.

Believe then that your word is to be acted upon by an Almighty Power; feel its great reality, in and through all things you speak into it; and declare just what you wish it to do for you, never doubting in your own mind but that it will do just as you have directed.

All that a practitioner has to do is to convince himself, to know, to believe, and that thing will happen to him which he states. One of the first things, then, is to be definite; to have a mental likeness of the thing that you desire; to know exactly what you want. This mental likeness, this absolute acceptance of the fact that it now is, must never be overlooked; without it you will not accomplish.

We sit down of our own souls, at peace with the world, at peace with ourselves; we realize that we are dealing with something that is a reality, something that cannot fail. We try to get a clear concept of the thing; we rest in that realization, while the Universal Creative Power takes it up and acts upon it.

We have stated just what we wanted done unto us; we have believed; we have believed that we have received; never again will we contradict the fact that we have stated. The person who can do this is sure of getting results.

Understanding And Guidance

The inner man is always in immediate connection with the Infinite of understanding. We are immersed in a living intelligence; we are surrounded by a Power that knows, for "In Him we live and move and have our being."

If our outer thought were never confused, we should at all times draw from this Infinite source of knowledge; we should be guided by It and never make mistakes; our minds would be like the smooth surface of a lake, unruffled by wind and storm.

But with most of us this is not the case; we become confused in the outer so that the surface of the mind is in turmoil, no longer clear and transparent, and we cannot get the clear vision, the real guidance, and we get things wrong because we do not see clearly.

The development of the understanding is learning to draw from the Infinite understanding; we can never do this while we are confused in our thinking.

The first thing to do when we wish a greater understanding is to be still and listen to the inner voice, to withdraw for a few moments into the silence of the soul taking here what we already know, and realizing that a greater intelligence is enlarging it.

Here we indefinitely take the pattern of our thought, the thing that we are working on, and ask for, and receive, new light; we hold this up in Divine Light and try to believe that we are being guided; we state that Supreme Intelligence and Absolute Power are acting upon our thought and bringing it to pass; it is now guiding us and we shall make no mistake; we hold ourselves in the Secret Place of the Most High, and abide under the shadow of the Almighty.

How To Know Just What To Do

Often we find ourselves confronted by the problem of how to begin. We are not sure what we want to do; we see no way to begin anything; see nothing to begin on; when we find ourselves in this position, humanly speaking, not knowing where to turn, then of all times we must be quiet and listen; then of all times we must trust that the same power that *started all things* will also *start us* in the right road, for without some superior power we shall surely fail.

How often do people in the business world find themselves in this position. They realize that something must be done, but what? How get the idea to work out?

Here we must wait and know that the same power that first thought a universe into being can also think our world and work into being. It knows all things; it knows how to begin and it cannot fail; we wish in some way to connect with this power that will never fail us, so that we may draw from it some idea to begin with.

We must realize that there is something that wants to respond, to make manifest and in this realization wait for the idea; it may not come at first, but we must be patient, never doubting, and waiting thus in faith, it *will* come.

I once knew a business man who was connected with a firm that had always been very successful, but at that time something had occurred that was causing them to lose out. This had gone on for a year and things were going from bad to worse. Failure seemed inevitable. He became interested in New Thought. He was told he could draw an idea from the Infinite and work it out on the plane of the visible. He told his partners that he wished to go home for a few days and that when he came back he would have worked out an idea which would put the business on a successful basis. They laughed at him, as people generally laugh at something they do not understand, but having no other plan they gave their consent. He went home and for three days sat in deep thought, claiming Supreme guidance and absolute leading of the Spirit. During this time a complete plan formulated in his mind as to the exact method to pursue in the business. He returned and told his plan to his partners. Again they laughed, saying it could not be done in business; could not be done any way; it would not work. But again they consented, knowing it was this or failure. He then went to work carrying out all the details of his thought, following each leading that had come to him during those three days, and within a year he brought the failing business to a standard that transcended anything they had ever before experienced, He proved the law and became such an expert, that he gave up his business and devoted his entire time to helping other people do the same for themselves as he had done.

What this man did any one can do if he will follow the same course and refuse to become discouraged. There is a power that simply awaits our recognition of it, to spring into our thought as an unfailing leading, an unerring guidance. To those who lean on the ever outstretched arm of the Infinite, life is big with limitless possibilities. We must wait and listen, then go about our outer business with an inner conviction that we are being led into a more perfect expression of life. All can do this.

Following Up A Thought

When we feel that we do have the right leading; when that something inside us tells us that we are led; then, no matter what it appears like, we must follow it up. Something beyond our intelligence is doing the thing through us and we must do nothing to contradict it.

Perhaps it will cause us to do something that seems to go contrary to the experience of the race. This makes no difference. All advance in invention and all advance along any line has always gone ahead of what the experience of the race thinks is possible.

Great men are the ones who get a vision and then go to work to make it come true, never looking to one side but with one-pointedness and calm determination, stick to the thing until it is accomplished.

It may take much patience and a great deal of faith, but the end is as sure as is the reality of a Supreme Being itself.

Never hesitate to trust in that inner leading, never fear but it will be right. We are all in the midst of Supreme Intelligence; It presses against the doors of our thought, waiting to be known. We must be open to It at all times, ready to receive direction and to be guided into greater truths.

The Single Stream Of Thought

All That we create are all in Mind and what we think into it is taken up and done unto us.. This means that as we think it will be done. We cannot think one way one day and change our thought the next and hope to get the desired results. We must be very clear in our thought, sending out only such thoughts as we wish to see manifested in our condition.

Here is something worth remembering. Unless we are working with people who think as we do, we had better be working alone. One stream of thought, even though it may not be very powerful, will do more for us than many powerful streams that are at variance with each other. This means that, unless we are sure that we are working with people who harmonize, we would better work alone. Of course we cannot retire from business simply because people do not agree with us, but what we can do is to keep our thoughts to ourselves. We do not have to leave the world in order to control our thought; but we do have to learn that we can stay right in the world and still think just what we want to think, regardless of what others are thinking.

One single stream of thought, daily sent out into Creative Mind, will do wonders. Within a year the person who will practice this will have completely changed his conditions of life. The way to practice this is daily to spend some time in thinking and in mentally seeing just what is wanted; see the thing just as it is wished and then affirm that this is now done. Try to feel that what has been stated is the truth.

Words and affirmations simply give shape to thought; they are not creative. Feeling is creative and the more feeling that is put into the word the greater power it will have over conditions. In doing this we think of the condition only as an effect, something that follows what we think. It cannot help following our thought. This is the way that all creation comes into expression.

It is a great help to realize mentally that at all times a great stream of thought and power is operating through us; it is constantly going out into Mind, where it is taken up and acted upon. Our business is to keep that stream of thought just where we want it to be: to be ready at any time to act when the impulse comes for action. Our action must never be negative, it must always be affirmative, for we are dealing with something that cannot fail. We may fail to realize, but the power in itself is Infinite and cannot fail. We are setting in motion in the Absolute a stream of thought that will never cease until it accomplishes its purpose. Try to feel this, be filled with a great joy as you feel that it is given to you to use this great and only power.

Keep the thought clear and never worry about the way that things seem to be going. Let go of all outer conditions when working in Mind, for there is where things are made; there creation is going on, and it is now making something for us. This must be believed as never believed before; it must be known as the great reality; it must be felt as the only Presence. There is no other way to obtain.

Though all the Infinite may want to give, yet we must take, and, as far as we are concerned, that taking is mental. Though people may laugh at this, even that does not matter, "He laughs best who laughs last." We know in "What we believe," and that will be sufficient.

Enlarging Our Thought

We can never stand still in our thought. Either we will be growing or else we will be going back. As we can attract to ourselves only what we first have a mental likeness of, it follows that if we wish to attract larger things we must provide larger thoughts. This enlarging of consciousness is so necessary that too much cannot be said about it.

Most people get only a short way and then stop: they cannot seem to get beyond a certain point; they can do so much and no more. Why is it that a person in business does just about so much each year? We see people in all walks of life, getting so far, never going beyond a certain point. There must be a reason for everything; nothing happens, if all is governed by law, and we can come to no other conclusion.

When we look into the mental reason for things we find out why things happen. The man who gets so far and never seems to go beyond that point is still governed by law; when he allows his thoughts to take him out into larger fields of action, his conditions come up to his thought; when he stops enlarging his thought he stops growing. If he would still keep on in thought, realizing more and still more, he would find that in the outer form of things he would be doing greater things.

There are many reasons why a man stops thinking larger things. One of them is a lack of imagination. He cannot conceive of anything more to follow than that which has already happened. Another thought works like this: "This is as far as any one can go in my business." Right here he signs his own death warrant. Often a person will say, "I am too old to do bigger things." There he stops. Someone else will say, "Competition is too great"; and here is where this man stops; he can go no further than his thought will carry him.

All this is unnecessary when we realize that life is first of all Consciousness, and then conditions follow. We see no reason why a man should not go on and on, and never stop growing. No matter what age or what circumstance, if life is thought, we can keep on thinking bigger things. There is no reason why a man who is already doing well should not be able mentally to conceive of a still better condition. What if we are active? There is always a greater activity possible. We can still see a little beyond what has come before. This is just what we should do, see, even though it be but a little beyond our former thought. If we always practice this, we will find that every year we shall be growing, every month we shall be advancing; and as time goes on we shall become really great. As there is no stopping in that power which is Infinite, as the Limitless is without bounds, so should we keep on trying to see more and greater possibilities in life.

We should definitely work every day for the expansion of thought. If we have fifty customers a day we should endeavor to believe that we have sixty. When we have sixty we should mentally see seventy. This should never stop; there is no stopping place in mind.

Let go of everything else, drop everything else from your thought, and mentally see more coming to you than has ever come before; believe that Mind is establishing this unto you, and then go about your business in the regular way. Never see the limitation; never dwell upon it, and above all things else never talk limitation to any one; this is the only way, and there is no other way to grow a larger thought. The man with the big thought is always the man who does big things in life. Get hold of the biggest thing that you can think of and claim it for your own; mentally see it and hold it as a thing already done, and you will prove to yourself that life is without bounds.

Always Be Gathering

There is no reason why a person should ever stop.

This does not mean that we should be miserly, trying to accumulate more and more to hold, but that our thought should so enlarge that it can not help gathering more and more, even though, on the other hand, or with the other hand, we are ever distributing that which we gather. Indeed, the only reason for having is that we may give out of that which we have.

No matter what big thing happens to us we should still be expecting more and more. Even when we think that we have at last arrived; right at the moment when it seems as though life had given us all that we could stand; right here let it be but a beginning for still greater things.

No matter how large the picture that you hold in mind, make it larger. The reason why so many people come to the point where they stop is that they come to a point where they stop growing in their own minds. They come to a point where they can see no more, thinking that because they have really done a big thing they should stop there. We must watch our thought for signs of inactivity. Nothing in the universe ever stops. Everything is built on a boundless basis, drawn from a limitless source, come forth from an Infinite sea of unmanifest life We speak forth into this life and draw back from it all that we first think into it. Life is always limitless, and the only thing that limits us is our inability to conceive mentally, and we should draw more and more from that limitless source.

Mental Likeness

We can draw from the Infinite only as much as we first think into it. It is at this point that so many fail, thinking that all they need to do is to affirm what they want and it will follow. While it is true that affirmations have real power, it is also true that they have only that which we speak into them.

As we cannot speak a word that we do not know, so we cannot make an affirmation that we do not understand. We really affirm only that which we know to be true; we know that to be true which we have experienced within ourselves. Although we may have heard or read that this or that thing is true, it is only when there is something within our own souls that corresponds or recognizes its truth, that it is true to us. This ought never to be lost sight of: we can effectively affirm only that which we know, and we know only that which we are. It is herein that we see the necessity of providing within a greater concept of life; a bigger idea of ourselves and a more expanded concept of the Universe in which we live, move and have our being. This is a matter of inner growth together with the enlarging of all lines of thought and activity.

If we want to do a thing that is really worth doing, we must mentally grow until we are that thing, which we want to see made flesh. This may take time, but we should be glad to use all the time necessary to our own development.

But few people in limitation have a mental likeness of plenty. This likeness must be provided. The thought mast be large enough to cover the whole of the thing desired; a small thought will produce only a small thing. The very fact that all is Mind proves this to be true. All *is* mind and, because it is, we can draw from that mind only that which we first think into it as a reality. We must become the thing we want. We must see it, think it, realize it, before the creative power of Mind can work it out for us. This is an inner process of the expansion of consciousness. It is a thought, growing and realizing within. All can do this who wish and who will take the time and trouble, but it will mean work. The majority of people are too lazy to make the effort.

Daily we must train our thought to see that only which we wish to experience, and since we are growing into what we are mentally dwelling upon, we should put all small and insignificant thoughts and ideals out of our thinking and see things in a larger way. We must cultivate the habit of an enlarged mental horizon, daily seeing farther and farther ahead, and so experiencing larger and greater things in our daily life.

A good practice for the enlargement of thought is daily to see ourselves in a little bigger place, filled with more of activity, surrounded with increased influence and power; feel more and more that things are coming to us; see that much more is just ahead, and so far as possible, know that we now have all that we see and all that we feel. Affirm that you are that larger thing; that you are now entered into that larger life; feel that something within is drawing more to you; live with the idea and let the concept grow, expecting only the biggest and the best to happen. Never let small thoughts come into your mind, and you will soon find that a larger and greater experience has come into your life.

Keeping The Thing In Mind

Never let go of the mental image until it becomes manifested. Daily bring up the clear picture of what is wanted and impress it on the mind as an accomplished fact. This impressing on our own minds the thought of what we wish to realize will cause our own minds to impress the same thought on Universal Mind. In this way we shall be praying without ceasing. We do not have to hold continually the thought of something we want in order to get it, but the thought that we may inwardly become the thing we want. Fifteen minutes, twice each day, is time enough to spend in order to demonstrate anything, but the rest of the time ought also to be spent constructively. That is, we must stop all negative thinking and give over all wrong thought, holding fast to the realization that it is now done unto us. We must know that we are dealing with the only power there is in the Universe; that there is none other beside it, and that we are in it partaking of its nature and its laws. Always, behind the word that we send forth, must be the calm confidence in our ability to speak into the power, and the willingness of Mind to execute for us. We must gradually grow in confidence and in trust in the unseen world of spiritual activity. This is not hard, if we but remember that the Spirit makes things out of Itself by simply becoming the thing that it makes, and since there is no other power to oppose it, it will always work. The Spirit will never fail us if we never fail to believe in its goodness and its responsiveness.

Life will become one grand song, when we realize that since God is for us, none can be against us. We shall cease merely to exist; we shall live.

Destroy All Thoughts That We Do Not Wish To Experience

We must resolutely set our faces to the rising consciousness of the Son of Truth; seeing only the One Power we must destroy the adversary and leave the field to God or Good. All that is in any way negative must be wiped off the slate and we must daily come into the higher thought, to be washed clean of the dust and chaos of the objective life. In the silence of the soul's communion with the Great Cause of All Being, into the stillness of the Absolute, into the secret place of the Most High, back of the din and the ceaseless roar of life, we shall find a resting place and a place of real spiritual power. Speak in this inner silence and say, "I am one with the Almighty; I am one with all life, with all power, with all presence. I AM, I AM, I AM." Listen to the silence. From out of the seeming void the voice of peace will answer the waiting soul, "All is well."

Here we make known all our needs and wants, and here we receive first hand from the Infinite all that we shall ever need to make life healthy, happy and harmonious. Few enter here, because of the belief that conditions and circumstances control. Know that there is no law but God's law; that the soul sets its own law in the Infinite and that our slightest wish is honored of the Father Mind.

Daily practice the truth and daily die to all error-thought. Spend more time receiving and realizing the, presence of the Most High and less time worrying. Wonderful power will come to the one who believes and trusts in that Power in which he has come to believe. Know that all good and all God is with you; All Life and All Power; and never again say, "I fear," but always, "I trust, because 'I know in whom I have believed.'"

Direct Practice For Prosperity

Suppose that you are doing a mail order business and sending out cards to the whole country. Take the cards into your hands, or simply think of them and declare into the only Mind that they will accomplish that for which they are sent out; know that every word written on them is truth and carries its own conviction with it; see them each reaching that place where it will be received with gladness and read with interest; declare this to be so now; feel it to be the truth; mentally assert that each card will find its way to the exact place where it will be wanted and where it will benefit the receiver; feel that each card is cared for by the Spirit; that it is a messenger of truth and power and that it will carry conviction and realization with it. When the word is .spoken always feel that Mind at once takes it up and never fails to act upon it. Our place in the creative order is to know this and to be willing to do all that we can without hurry or worry, and, above all else, to trust absolutely in the Spirit to do the rest. He who sees most clearly and believes most implicitly will make the greatest demonstration. This one should be you, and will be you as soon as the false thought is gone and the realization that there is but the one power and the one presence comes. We are wrapped in an Infinite Love and Intelligence and we should cover ourselves with it and claim its protection from all evil. Declare that your word is the presence and the activity of the Power of all that is and wait for the perfect concept to unfold.

Race Consciousness

One of the things which greatly hinders us from demonstrating a greater degree of prosperity we may call race thought or race consciousness. This is the result of all that the race has thought or believed. We are immersed in it, and those who are receptive to it are controlled by it. All thought seeks expression along the lines of least resistance. When we become negative or fearful we attract that kind of thought and condition. We must be sure of ourselves; we must be positive; we must not be aggressive, but absolutely sure and poised within. Negative people are always picking up negative conditions; they get into trouble easily: Persons who are positive draw positive things; they are always successful. Few people realize that the law of thought is the great reality; that thoughts produce things. When we come to understand this power of thought, we will carefully watch our thinking to see that no thought enters that we should not want made into a thing.

We can guard our minds by knowing that no negative thought can enter; we can daily practice by saying that no race thought of limitation can enter the mind; that Spirit forms itself around us and protects us from all fear and from all limitation. Let us clothe ourselves in the great realization that all power is ours and that nothing else can enter; let us fill the atmosphere of our homes, and places of business with streams of positive thought. Other people will feel this and will like to be near us and enter into the things that we enter into. In this way we shall be continually drawing only the best.

Developing Intuition

If a person always lived near to mind he would never make any great mistakes. Some seem to have the faculty of always knowing just what is best to do; they always succeed because they avoid making errors. We can all so train ourselves that we will be guided by the Supreme Mind of the Universe; but we can never do this until we believe that we can receive direct from the source of all knowledge. This is done by sitting in the silence and knowing that the Spirit is inwardly directing us. We should try to feel that our thought is being permeated by the thought of the Spirit. We should expect it to direct but should never become discouraged if at once a direct impression is not received. The work is going on even if it is not seen or even felt. Thought is forming in our mind and in time will come forth as an idea. When the idea does come always trust in it even though it may not seem to be quite as we had expected. The first impressions are usually the most direct and the clearest; they are generally direct from the Mind of the Universe and should be carefully worked out into expression.

We declare as we sit in the silence that the Spirit of all knowledge is making known within us just what we should do; that it is telling us just what to say or where to go. Have absolute reliance on this as it is one of the most important things to do. We should always get that inner assurance before undertaking any new enterprise; being sure that we have really put the whole thing into the hands of life and that all that we have to do is to work it out in the outer. We shall learn to avoid mistakes when we learn to be directed by that inner voice that never makes mistakes. We should declare in the silence that intelligence is guiding us and it will do so.

Presence Of Activity

Suppose that your place of business does not seem to manifest any activity; that is, suppose that customers do not come. To the person in the business world the presence of customers generally means activity. Suppose that you have come to believe that the principle will work in the smallest as well as in the greatest things. What you want now is a greater activity. How are you going to see activity when there is none?

Here is a great question in Truth. Must we overlook that which we see, and that which we have experienced? Yes, absolutely; there is no other way. If we keep on seeing the thing as it appears we will never be able to change its appearance. What we must do, then, in spite of the seeming inactivity, is still to know and mentally to see and declare that we are in the midst of activity. Feel this to be true; mentally see the place crowded; know that it is packed full of customers all the time; declare that your word draws them in; have no sense of strain about it whatever; simply know that you are dealing with the only power that there is; it will work; it must work. Realize when you have spoken the word that a greater power has taken it up and that it is being established unto you. Have no idea of limitation; speak forth into mind with perfect trust. If you have the ability mentally to see the place full, combine this with the word, and daily visualize it as being filled. Always combine faith in the higher power with all that you do; feel that you are being especially looked after. This is true. When a soul turns to the Universe of unmanifest life, at the same time It turns toward him. Jesus told this in the story of the Prodigal Son; the Father saw him afar off. Always there is that inward turning to us of the Parent Mind when we turn to It and place ourselves in closer contact with Life.

We must keep our mind clear so that when the Spirit brings the gift we will be open to receive it. Even God cannot force things upon us. We must receive even before we see.

> ”For the feeble hands and helpless,
> Groping blindly in the darkness
> Touch God's right hand in that darkness
> And are lifted up and strengthened.”

Always, when we believe, we will have that belief honored of the Spirit of Life. Mentally seeing just what we want; still seeing even though the heavens fall, we shall succeed in proving that the law of life is a law of liberty. God made man to have all that the Universe contained and then left him alone to discover his own nature.

Stop all striving and all struggle and within your own soul know the truth and trust absolutely in it. Daily declare that you are being guided and protected and that the power of the Spirit is bringing all to pass, and wait in perfect peace and confidence. Such an attitude of mind will overcome anything and will prove that spiritual thought force is the only real power in the Universe.

Drawing Your Own To You

Suppose that you wish to draw friends and companions to you; that you wish to enlarge your circle of friendships. This, too, can all be worked out by law, for everything can be worked out by the same law, the reason being that all is One and that the One becomes the many in expression. There are too many people in the world who are lonesome because they have a sense of separation from people. The thing to do is not to try to unify with people, but *with the Principle of Life* behind all people and things. This is working from the center and not the circumference; in this One Mind are the minds of all people. When you unite your thought with the whole you will be united with the parts of the whole. The first thing to do, then, is to realize that Life is your friend and companion; feel the divine companionship; feel that you are one with all life; declare that, as this thought awakens within your mind, so does it awaken within the mind of the whole race; feel that the world is being drawn to you; love the world and everyone who is in it; include all, if you would be included in all. The world seeks strength; be strong. The world loves love; embody it; see the good in all people; let go of all else. People will feel your love and will be drawn into it. Love is the greatest power in the Universe; it is at the base of all else; it is the cause of all that is. Feel your love to be like a great light lighting the pathway of the whole world; it will come back to you bringing so many friends that there will not be time enough to enjoy them all. Become a real friend and you will have many friends.

Be sufficient unto yourself and at the same time include all else, and people will feel your strength and will have a desire to come into the radiance of it. Never become unhappy or morbid; always be cheerful and radiate good nature and happiness; never look depressed or down in the mouth; the world is attracted to the strongest center of cheer and good fellowship. Never allow your feelings to be hurt. No one wants to hurt you, and none could, even though they did want to; you are above all that. Wherever you go know that the Spirit of Truth goes before and prepares the way, bringing to you every friend and influence that will be necessary to your comfort and well being. This is not selfishness but good sense and will surely bring to you a harvest of friends and companions.

Declare unto Mind that you are now linked with all people and that all people are linked with you: see yourself surrounded with hosts of friends; mentally feel their presence and rejoice that all good is yours now. Do this no matter what seems to happen, and it will not be long before you will meet wonderful friends and will be brought into touch with the great of the world.

The Final Word

In the last analysis, man is just what he thinks himself to be; he is big in capacity if he thinks big thoughts; he is small if he thinks small thoughts. He will attract to himself what he thinks most about. He can learn to govern his own destiny when he learns to control his thoughts. In order to do this he must first realize that everything in the manifest universe is the result of some inner activity of Mind. This Mind is God, producing a universe by the activity of His own divine thoughts; man is in this Mind as a thinking center, and what he thinks governs his life, even as God's thought governs the Universe, by setting in motion all the cosmic activities. This is so easy to understand, and so plain as to use that we often wonder why we have been so long finding out this, the greatest of all truths of all the ages. Believing; thinking what is believed to be true; thinking into Mind each day that which is wished to be returned; eliminating negative thoughts; holding all positive thoughts; giving thanks to the Spirit of Life that it is so trusting always in the higher law; never arguing with one's self or with others; using; these are the steps which, when followed, will bring us to where we shall not have to ask if it be true, for, having demonstrated, we shall know.

The seed that falls into the ground shall bear fruit of its own kind; and nothing shall hinder it. "He that hath ears to hear, let him hear."

The Science of Getting Rich

Preface

This book is pragmatical, not philosophical; a practical manual, not a treatise upon theories. It is intended for the men and women whose most pressing need is for money; who wish to get rich first, and philosophize afterward. It is for those who have, so far, found neither the time, the means, nor the opportunity to go deeply into the study of metaphysics, but who want results and who are willing to take the conclusions of science as a basis for action, without going into all the processes by which those conclusions were reached.

It is expected that the reader will take the fundamental statements upon faith, just as he would take statements concerning a law of electrical action if they were promulgated by a Marconi or an Edison; and, taking the statements upon faith, that he will prove their truth by acting upon them without fear or hesitation. Every man or woman who does this will certainly get rich; for the science herein applied is an exact science, and failure is impossible. For the benefit, however, of those who wish to investigate philosophical theories and so secure a logical basis for faith, I will here cite certain authorities.

The monistic theory of the universe the theory that One is All, and that All is One; That one Substance manifests itself as the seeming many elements of the material world -is of Hindu origin, and has been gradually winning its way into the thought of the western world for two hundred years. It is the foundation of all the Oriental philosophies, and of those of Descartes, Spinoza, Leibnitz, Schopenhauer, Hegel, and Emerson.

The reader who would dig to the philosophical foundations of this is advised to read Hegel and Emerson for himself.

In writing this book I have sacrificed all other considerations to plainness and simplicity of style, so that all might understand. The plan of action laid down herein was deduced from the conclusions of philosophy; it has been thoroughly tested, and bears the supreme test of practical experiment; it works. If you wish to know how the conclusions were arrived at, read the writings of the authors mentioned above; and if you wish to reap the fruits of their philosophies in actual practice, read this book and do exactly as it tells you to do---

The Author

Chapter 1: The Right To Be Rich

Whatever may be said in praise of poverty, the fact remains that it is not possible to live a really complete or successful life unless one is rich. No man can rise to his greatest possible height in talent or soul development unless he has plenty of money; for to unfold the soul and to develop talent he must have many things to use, and he cannot have these things unless he has money to buy them with.

A man develops in mind, soul, and body by making use of things, and society is so organized that man must have money in order to become the possessor of things; therefore, the basis of all advancement for man must be the science of getting rich.

The object of all life is development; and everything that lives has an inalienable right to all the development it is capable of attaining.

Man's right to life means his right to have the free and unrestricted use of all the things which may be necessary to his fullest mental, spiritual, and physical unfoldment; or, in other words, his right to be rich.

In this book, I shall not speak of riches in a figurative way; to be really rich does not mean to be satisfied or contented with a little. No man ought to be satisfied with a little if he is capable of using and enjoying more. The purpose of Nature is the advancement and unfoldment of life; and every man should have all that can contribute to the power, elegance, beauty, and richness of life; to be content with less is sinful.

The man who owns all he wants for the living of all the life he is capable of living is rich; and no man who has not plenty of money can have all he wants. Life has advanced so far, and become so complex, that even the most ordinary man or woman requires a great amount of wealth in order to live in a manner that even approaches completeness. Every person naturally wants to become all that they are capable of becoming; this desire to realize innate possibilities is inherent in human nature; we cannot help wanting to be all that we can be. Success in life is becoming what you want to be; you can become what you want to be only by making use of things, and you can have the free use of things only as you become rich enough to buy them. To understand the science of getting rich is therefore the most essential of all knowledge.

There is nothing wrong in wanting to get rich. The desire for riches is really the desire for a richer, fuller, and more abundant life; and that desire is praise worthy. The man who does not desire to live more abundantly is abnormal, and so the man who does not desire to have money enough to buy all he wants is abnormal.

There are three motives for which we live; we live for the body, we live for the mind, we live for the soul. No one of these is better or holier than the other; all are alike desirable, and no one of the three--body, mind, or soul--can live fully if either of the others is cut short of full life and expression. It is not right or noble to live only for the soul and deny mind or body; and it is wrong to live for the intellect and deny body or soul.

We are all acquainted with the loathsome consequences of living for the body and denying both mind and soul; and we see that real life means the complete expression of all that man can give forth through body, mind, and soul. Whatever he can say, no man can be really happy or satisfied unless his body is living fully in every function, and unless the same is true of his mind and his soul. Wherever there is unexpressed possibility, or function not performed, there is unsatisfied desire. Desire is possibility seeking expression, or function seeking performance.

Man cannot live fully in body without good food, comfortable clothing, and warm shelter; and without freedom from excessive toil. Rest and recreation are also necessary to his physical life.

He cannot live fully in mind without books and time to study them, without opportunity for travel and observation, or without intellectual companionship.

To live fully in mind he must have intellectual recreations, and must surround himself with all the objects of art and beauty he is capable of using and appreciating.

To live fully in soul, man must have love; and love is denied expression by poverty.

A man's highest happiness is found in the bestowal of benefits on those he loves; love finds its most natural and spontaneous expression in giving. The man who has nothing to give cannot fill his place as a husband or father, as a citizen, or as a man. It is in the use of material things that a man finds full life for his body, develops his mind, and unfolds his soul. It is therefore of supreme importance to him that he should be rich.

It is perfectly right that you should desire to be rich; if you are a normal man or woman you cannot help doing so. It is perfectly right that you should give your best attention to the Science of Getting Rich, for it is the noblest and most necessary of all studies. If you neglect this study, you are derelict in your duty to yourself, to God and humanity; for you can render to God and humanity no greater service than to make the most of yourself.

Chapter 2: There is A Science of Getting Rich

There is a Science of getting rich, and it is an exact science, like algebra or arithmetic. There are certain laws which govern the process of acquiring riches; once these laws are learned and obeyed by any man, he will get rich with mathematical certainty.

The ownership of money and property comes as a result of doing things in a certain way; those who do things in this Certain Way, whether on purpose or accidentally, get rich; while those who do not do things in this Certain Way, no matter how hard they work or how able they are, remain poor.

It is a natural law that like causes always produce like effects; and, therefore, any man or woman who learns to do things in this certain way will infallibly get rich.

That the above statement is true is shown by the following facts:

Getting rich is not a matter of environment, for, if it were, all the people in certain neighborhoods would become wealthy; the people of one city would all be rich, while those of other towns would all be poor; or the inhabitants of one state would roll in wealth, while those of an adjoining state would be in poverty.

But everywhere we see rich and poor living side by side, in the same environment, and often engaged in the same vocations. When two men are in the same locality, and in the same business, and one gets rich while the other remains poor, it shows that getting rich is not, primarily, a matter of environment. Some environments may be more favorable than others, but when two men in the same business are in the same neighborhood, and one gets rich while the other fails, it indicates that getting rich is the result of doing things in a Certain Way.

And further, the ability to do things in this certain way is not due solely to the possession of talent, for many people who have great talent remain poor, while other who have very little talent get rich.

Studying the people who have got rich, we find that they are an average lot in all respects, having no greater talents and abilities than other men. It is evident that they do not get rich because they possess talents and abilities that other men have not, but because they happen to do things in a Certain Way.

Getting rich is not the result of saving, or "thrift"; many very penurious people are poor, while free spenders often get rich.

Nor is getting rich due to doing things which others fail to do; for two men in the same business often do almost exactly the same things, and one gets rich while the other remains poor or becomes bankrupt.

From all these things, we must come to the conclusion that getting rich is the result of doing things in a Certain Way.

If getting rich is the result of doing things in a Certain Way, and if like causes always produce like effects, then any man or woman who can do things in that way can become rich, and the whole matter is brought within the domain of exact science.

The question arises here, whether this Certain Way may not be so difficult that only a few may follow it. This cannot be true, as we have seen, so far as natural ability is concerned. Talented people get rich, and blockheads get rich; intellectually brilliant people get rich, and very stupid people get rich; physically strong people get rich, and weak and sickly people get rich.

Some degree of ability to think and understand is, of course, essential; but in so far natural ability is concerned, any man or woman who has sense enough to read and understand these words can certainly get rich.

Also, we have seen that it is not a matter of environment. Location counts for something; one would not go to the heart of the Sahara and expect to do successful business. Getting rich involves the necessity of dealing with men, and of being where there are people to deal with; and if these people are inclined to deal in the way you want to deal, so much the better. But that is about as far as environment goes.

If anybody else in your town can get rich, so can you; and if anybody else in your state can get rich, so can you.

Again, it is not a matter of choosing some particular business or profession. People get rich in every business, and in every profession; while their next door neighbors in the same vocation remain in poverty.

It is true that you will do best in a business which you like, and which is congenial to you; and if you have certain talents which are well developed, you will do best in a business which calls for the exercise of those talents.

Also, you will do best in a business which is suited to your locality; an ice-cream parlor would do better in a warm climate than in Greenland, and a salmon fishery will succeed better in the Northwest than in Florida, where there are no salmon.

But, aside from these general limitations, getting rich is not dependent upon your engaging in some particular business, but upon your learning to do things in a Certain Way. If you are now in business, and anybody else in your locality is getting rich in the same business, while you are not getting rich, it is because you are not doing things in the same Way that the other person is doing them.

No one is prevented from getting rich by lack of capital. True, as you get capital the increase becomes more easy and rapid; but one who has capital is already rich, and does not need to consider how to become so. No matter how poor you may be, if you begin to do things in the Certain Way you will begin to get rich; and you will begin to have capital. The getting of capital is a part of the process of getting rich; and it is a part of the result which invariably follows the doing of things in the Certain Way. You may be the poorest man on the continent, and be deeply in debt; you may have neither friends, influence, nor resources; but if you begin to do things in this way, you must infallibly begin to get rich, for like causes must produce like effects. If you have no capital, you can get capital; if you are in the wrong business, you can get into the right business; if you are in the wrong location, you can go to the right location; and you can do so by beginning in your present business and in your present location to do things in the Certain Way which causes success.

Chapter 3: Is Opportunity Monopolized?

No man is kept poor because opportunity has been taken away from him; because other people have monopolized the wealth, and have put a fence around it. You may be shut off from engaging in business in certain lines, but there are other channels open to you. Probably it would be hard for you to get control of any of the great railroad systems; that field is pretty well monopolized. But the electric railway business is still in its infancy, and offers plenty of scope for enterprise; and it will be but a very few years until traffic and transportation through the air will become a great industry, and in all its branches will give employment to hundreds of thousands, and perhaps to millions, of people. Why not turn your attention to the development of aerial transportation, instead of competing with J.J. Hill and others for a chance in the steam railway world?

It is quite true that if you are a workman in the employ of the steel trust you have very little chance of becoming the owner of the plant in which you work; but it is also true that if you will commence to act in a Certain Way, you can soon leave the employ of the steel trust; you can buy a farm of from ten to forty acres, and engage in business as a producer of foodstuffs. There is great opportunity at this time for men who will live upon small tracts of land and cultivate the same intensively; such men will certainly get rich. You may say that it is impossible for you to get the land, but I am going to prove to you that it is not impossible, and that you can certainly get a farm if you will go to work in a Certain Way.

At different periods the tide of opportunity sets in different directions, according to the needs of the whole, and the particular stage of social evolution which has been reached. At present, in America, it is setting toward agriculture and the allied industries and professions. To-day, opportunity is open before the factory worker in his line. It is open before the business man who supplies the farmer more than before the one who supplies the factory worker; and before the professional man who waits upon the farmer more than before the one who serves the working class.

There is abundance of opportunity for the man who will go with the tide, instead of trying to swim against it.

So the factory workers, either as individuals or as a class, are not deprived of opportunity. The workers are not being "kept down" by their masters; they are not being "ground" by the trusts and combinations of capital. As a class, they are where they are because they do not do things in a Certain Way. If the workers of America chose to do so, they could follow the example of their brothers in Belgium and other countries, and establish great department stores and co-operative industries; they could elect men of their own class to office, and pass laws favoring the development of such co-operative industries; and in a few years they could take peaceable possession of the industrial field.

The working class may become the master class whenever they will begin to do things in a Certain Way; the law of wealth is the same for them as it is for all others. This they must learn; and they will remain where they are as long as they continue to do as they do. The individual worker, however, is not held down by the ignorance or the mental slothfulness of his class; he can follow the tide of opportunity to riches, and this book will tell him how.

No one is kept in poverty by a shortness in the supply of riches; there is more than enough for all. A palace as large as the capitol at Washington might be built for every family on earth from the building material in the United States alone; and under intensive cultivation, this country would produce wool, cotton, linen, and silk enough to cloth each person in the world finer than Solomon was arrayed in all his glory; together with food enough to feed them all luxuriously.

The visible supply is practically inexhaustible; and the invisible supply really *is* inexhaustible.

Everything you see on earth is made from one original substance, out of which all things proceed.

New Forms are constantly being made, and older ones are dissolving; but all are shapes assumed by One Thing.

There is no limit to the supply of Formless Stuff, or Original Substance. The universe is made out of it; but it was not all used in making the universe. The spaces in, through, and between the forms of the visible universe are permeated and filled with the Original Substance; with the formless Stuff; with the raw material of all things. Ten thousand times as much as has been made might still be made, and even then we should not have exhausted the supply of universal raw material.

No man, therefore, is poor because nature is poor, or because there is not enough to go around.

Nature is an inexhaustible storehouse of riches; the supply will never run short. Original Substance is alive with creative energy, and is constantly producing more forms. When the supply of building material is exhausted, more will be produced; when the soil is exhausted so that food stuffs and materials for clothing will no longer grow upon it, it will be renewed or more soil will be made. When all the gold and silver has been dug from the earth, if man is still in such a stage of social development that he needs gold and silver, more will produced from the Formless. The Formless Stuff responds to the needs of man; it will not let him be without any good thing.

This is true of man collectively; the race as a whole is always abundantly rich, and if individuals are poor, it is because they do not follow the Certain Way of doing things which makes the individual man rich.

The Formless Stuff is intelligent; it is stuff which thinks. It is alive, and is always impelled toward more life.

It is the natural and inherent impulse of life to seek to live more; it is the nature of intelligence to enlarge itself, and of consciousness to seek to extend its boundaries and find fuller expression. The universe of forms has been made by Formless Living Substance, throwing itself into form in order to express itself more fully.

The universe is a great Living Presence, always moving inherently toward more life and fuller functioning.

Nature is formed for the advancement of life; its impelling motive is the increase of life. For this cause, everything which can possibly minister to life is bountifully provided; there can be no lack unless God is to contradict himself and nullify his own works.

You are not kept poor by lack in the supply of riches; it is a fact which I shall demonstrate a little farther on that even the resources of the Formless Supply are at the command of the man or woman who will act and think in a Certain Way.

Chapter 4: The First Principle in The Science of Getting Rich

Thought is the only power which can produce tangible riches from the Formless Substance. The stuff from which all things are made is a substance which thinks, and a thought of form in this substance produces the form.

Original Substance moves according to its thoughts; every form and process you see in nature is the visible expression of a thought in Original Substance. As the Formless Stuff thinks of a form, it takes that form; as it thinks of a motion, it makes that motion. That is the way all things were created. We live in a thought world, which is part of a thought universe. The thought of a moving universe extended throughout Formless Substance, and the Thinking Stuff moving according to that thought, took the form of systems of planets, and maintains that form. Thinking Substance takes the form of its thought, and moves according to the thought. Holding the idea of a circling system of suns and worlds, it takes the form of these bodies, and moves them as it thinks. Thinking the form of a slow-growing oak tree, it moves accordingly, and produces the tree, though centuries may be required to do the work. In creating, the Formless seems to move according to the lines of motion it has established; the thought of an oak tree does not cause the instant formation of a full-grown tree, but it does start in motion the forces which will produce the tree, along established lines of growth.

Every thought of form, held in thinking Substance, causes the creation of the form, but always, or at least generally, along lines of growth and action already established.

The thought of a house of a certain construction, if it were impressed upon Formless Substance, might not cause the instant formation, of the house; but it would cause the turning of creative energies already working in trade and commerce into such channels as to result in the speedy building of the house. And if there were no existing channels through which the creative energy could work, then the house would be formed directly from primal substance, without waiting for the slow processes of the organic and inorganic world.

No thought of form can be impressed upon Original Substance without causing the creation of the form.

Man is a thinking center, and can originate thought. All the forms that man fashions with his hands must first exist in his thought; he cannot shape a thing until he has thought that thing. And so far man has confined his efforts wholly to the work of his hands; he has applied manual labor to the world of forms, seeking to change or modify those already existing. He has never thought of trying to cause the creation of new forms by impressing his thoughts upon Formless Substance.

When man has a thought-form, he takes material from the forms of nature, and makes an image of the form which is in his mind. He has, so far, made little or no effort to co-operate with Formless Intelligence; to work "with the Father." He has not dreamed that he can "do what he seeth the Father doing." Man reshapes and modifies existing forms by manual labor;

he has given no attention to the question whether he may not produce things from Formless Substance by communicating his thoughts to it. We propose to prove that he may do so; to prove that any man or woman may do so, and to show how. As our first step, we must lay down three fundamental propositions.

First, we assert that there is one original formless stuff, or substance, from which all things are made. All the seemingly many elements are but different presentations of one element; all the many forms found in organic and inorganic nature are but different shapes, made from the same stuff. And this stuff is thinking stuff; a thought held in it produces the form of the thought. Thought, in thinking substance, produces shapes. Man is a thinking center, capable of original thought; if man can communicate his thought to original thinking substance, he can cause the creation, or formation, of the thing he thinks about. To summarize this:-

There is a thinking stuff from which all things are made, and which, in its original state, permeates, penetrates, and fills the interspaces of the universe.

A thought, in this substance, Produces the thing that is imaged by the thought.

Man can form things in his thought, and, by impressing his thought upon formless substance, can cause the thing he thinks about to be created.

It may be asked if I can prove these statements; and without going into details, I answer that I can do so, both by logic and experience.

Reasoning back from the phenomena of form and thought, I come to one original thinking substance; and reasoning forward from this thinking substance, I come to man's power to cause the formation of the thing he thinks about.

And by experiment, I find the reasoning true; and this is my strongest proof.

If one man who reads this book gets rich by doing what it tells him to do, that is evidence in support of my claim; but if every man who does what it tells him to do gets rich, that is positive proof until some one goes through the process and fails. The theory is true until the process fails; and this process will not fail, for every man who does exactly what this book tells him to do will get rich.

I have said that men get rich by doing things in a Certain Way; and in order to do so, men must become able to think in a certain way.

A man's way of doing things is the direct result of the way he thinks about things.

To do things in a way you want to do them, you will have to acquire the ability to think the way you want to think; this is the first step toward getting rich.

To think what you want to think is to think TRUTH, regardless of appearances.

Every man has the natural and inherent power to think what he wants to think, but it requires far more effort to do so than it does to think the thoughts which are suggested by appearances. To think according to appearance is easy; to think truth regardless of appearances is laborious, and requires the expenditure of more power than any other work man is called upon to perform.

There is no labor from which most people shrink as they do from that of sustained and consecutive thought; it is the hardest work in the world. This is especially true when truth is contrary to appearances. Every appearance in the visible world tends to produce a corresponding form in the mind which observes it; and this can only be prevented by holding the thought of the TRUTH.

To look upon the appearance of disease will produce the form of disease in your own mind, and ultimately in your body, unless you hold the thought of the truth, which is that there is no disease; it is only an appearance, and the reality is health.

To look upon the appearances of poverty will produce corresponding forms in your own mind, unless you hold to the truth that there is no poverty; there is only abundance.

To think health when surrounded by the appearances of disease, or to think riches when in the midst of appearances of poverty, requires power; but he who acquires this power becomes a MASTER MIND. He can conquer fate; he can have what he wants.

This power can only be acquired by getting hold of the basic fact which is behind all appearances; and that fact is that there is one Thinking Substance, from which and by which all things are made.

Then we must grasp the truth that every thought held in this substance becomes a form, and that man can so impress his thoughts upon it as to cause them to take form and become visible things.

When we realize this, we lose all doubt and fear, for we know that we can create what we want to create; we can get what we want to have, and can become what we want to be. As a first step toward getting rich, you must believe the three fundamental statements given previously in this chapter; and in order to emphasize them. I repeat them here:-

There is a thinking stuff from which all things are made, and which, in its original state, permeates, penetrates, and fills the interspaces of the universe.

A thought, in this substance, Produces the thing that is imaged by the thought.

Man can form things in his thought, and, by impressing his thought upon formless substance, can cause the thing he thinks about to be created.

You must lay aside all other concepts of the universe than this monistic one; and you must dwell upon this until it is fixed in your mind, and has become your habitual thought. Read these creed statements over and over again; fix every word upon your memory, and meditate upon them until you firmly believe what they say. If a doubt comes to you, cast it aside as a sin. Do not listen to arguments against this idea; do not go to churches or lectures where a contrary concept of things is taught or preached. Do not read magazines or books which teach a different idea; if you get mixed up in your faith, all your efforts will be in vain.

Do not ask why these things are true, nor speculate as to how they can be true; simply take them on trust.

The science of getting rich begins with the absolute acceptance of this faith.

Chapter 5: Increasing Life

You must get rid of the last vestige of the old idea that there is a Deity whose will it is that you should be poor, or whose purposes may be served by keeping you in poverty.

The Intelligent Substance which is All, and in All, and which lives in All and lives in you, is a consciously Living Substance. Being a consciously living substance, It must have the nature and inherent desire of every living intelligence for increase of life. Every living thing must continually seek for the enlargement of its life, because life, in the mere act of living, must increase itself.

A seed, dropped into the ground, springs into activity, and in the act of living produces a hundred more seeds; life, by living, multiplies itself. It is forever Becoming More; it must do so, if it continues to be at all.

Intelligence is under this same necessity for continuous increase. Every thought we think makes it necessary for us to think another thought; consciousness is continually expanding. Every fact we learn leads us to the learning of another fact; knowledge is continually increasing. Every talent we cultivate brings to the mind the desire to cultivate another talent; we are subject to the urge of life, seeking expression, which ever drives us on to know more, to do more, and to be more.

In order to know more, do more, and be more we must have more; we must have things to use, for we learn, and do, and become, only by using things. We must get rich, so that we can live more.

The desire for riches is simply the capacity for larger life seeking fulfillment; every desire is the effort of an unexpressed possibility to come into action. It is power seeking to manifest which causes desire. That which makes you want more money is the same as that which makes the plant grow; it is Life, seeking fuller expression.

The One Living Substance must be subject to this inherent law of all life; it is permeated with the desire to live more; that is why it is under the necessity of creating things.

The One Substance desires to live more in you; hence it wants you to have all the things you can use.

It is the desire of God that you should get rich. He wants you to get rich because he can express himself better through you if you have plenty of things to use in giving him expression. He can live more in you if you have unlimited command of the means of life.

The universe desires you to have everything you want to have.

Nature is friendly to your plans.

Everything is naturally for you.

Make up your mind that this is true.

It is essential, however that *your purpose should harmonize with the purpose that is in All.*

You must want real life, not mere pleasure of sensual gratification. Life is the performance of function; and the individual really lives only when he performs every function, physical, mental, and spiritual, of which he is capable, without excess in any.

You do not want to get rich in order to live swinishly, for the gratification of animal desires; that is not life. But the performance of every physical function is a part of life, and no one lives completely who denies the impulses of the body a normal and healthful expression.

You do not want to get rich solely to enjoy mental pleasures, to get knowledge, to gratify ambition, to outshine others, to be famous. All these are a legitimate part of life, but the man who lives for the pleasures of the intellect alone will only have a partial life, and he will never be satisfied with his lot.

You do not want to get rich solely for the good of others, to lose yourself for the salvation of mankind, to experience the joys of philanthropy and sacrifice. The joys of the soul are only a part of life; and they are no better or nobler than any other part.

You want to get rich in order that you may eat, drink, and be merry when it is time to do these things; in order that you may surround yourself with beautiful things, see distant lands, feed your mind, and develop your intellect; in order that you may love men and do kind things, and be able to play a good part in helping the world to find truth.

But remember that extreme altruism is no better and no nobler than extreme selfishness; both are mistakes.

Get rid of the idea that God wants you to sacrifice yourself for others, and that you can secure his favor by doing so; God requires nothing of the kind.

What he wants is that you should make the most of yourself, for yourself, and for others; and *you can help others more by making the most of yourself than in any other way.*

You can make the most of yourself only by getting rich; so it is right and praiseworthy that you should give your first and best thought to the work of acquiring wealth.

Remember, however, that the desire of Substance is for all, and its movements must be for more life to all; it cannot be made to work for less life to any, because it is equally in all, seeking riches and life.

Intelligent Substance will make things for you, but it will not take things away from some one else and give them to you.

You must get rid of the thought of competition. You are to create, not to compete for what is already created.

You do not have to take anything away from any one.

You do not have to drive sharp bargains.

You do not have to cheat, or to take advantage. You do not need to let any man work for you for less than he earns.

You do not have to covet the property of others, or to look at it with wishful eyes; no man has anything of which you cannot have the like, and that without taking what he has away from him.

You are to become a creator, not a competitor; you are going to get what you want, but in such a way that when you get it every other man will have more than he has now.

I am aware that there are men who get a vast amount of money by proceeding in direct opposition to the statements in the paragraph above, and may add a word of explanation here. Men of the plutocratic type, who become very rich, do so sometimes purely by their extraordinary ability on the plane of competition; and sometimes they unconsciously relate themselves to Substance in its great purposes and movements for the general racial upbuilding through industrial evolution. Rockefeller, Carnegie, Morgan, et al., have been the unconscious agents of the Supreme in the necessary work of systematizing and organizing productive industry; and in the end, their work will contribute immensely toward increased life for all. Their day is nearly over; they have organized production, and *will soon be succeeded by the agents of the multitude, who will organize the machinery of distribution.*

The multi-millionaires are like the monster reptiles of the prehistoric eras; they play a necessary part in the evolutionary process, but the same Power which produced them will dispose of them. And it is well to bear in mind that they have never been really rich; a record of the private lives of most of this class will show that they have really been the most abject and wretched of the poor.

Riches secured on the competitive plane are never satisfactory and permanent; they are yours to-day, and another's tomorrow. Remember, if you are to become rich in a scientific and certain way, you must rise entirely out of the competitive thought. You must never think for a moment that the supply is limited. Just as soon as you begin to think that all the money is being "cornered" and controlled by bankers and others, and that you must exert yourself to get laws passed to stop this process, and so on; in that moment you drop into the competitive mind, and your power to cause creation is gone for the time being; and what is worse, you will probably arrest the creative movements you have already instituted.

KNOW that there are countless millions of dollars' worth of gold in the mountains of the earth, not yet brought to light; and know that if there were not, more would be created from Thinking Substance to supply your needs.

KNOW that the money you need will come, even if it is necessary for a thousand men to be led to the discovery of new gold mines to-morrow.

Never look at the visible supply; look always at the limitless riches in Formless Substance, and KNOW that they are coming to you as fast as you can receive and use them. Nobody, by cornering the visible supply, can prevent you from getting what is yours.

So never allow yourself to think for an instant that all the best building spots will be taken before you get ready to build your house, unless you hurry. Never worry about the trusts and combines, and get anxious for fear they will soon come to own the whole earth. Never get afraid that you will lose what you want because some other person "beats you to it." That cannot possibly happen; you are not seeking any thing that is possessed by anybody else; you are causing what you want to be created from formless Substance, and the supply is without limits. Stick to the formulated statement:–

There is a thinking stuff from which all things are made, and which, in its original state, permeates, penetrates, and fills the interspaces of the universe.

A thought, in this substance, produces the thing that is imaged by the thought.

Man can form things in his thought, and, by impressing his thought upon formless substance, can cause the thing he thinks about to be created.

Chapter 6: How Riches Come to You

When I say that you do not have to drive sharp bargains, I do not mean that you do not have to drive any bargains at all, or that you are above the necessity for having any dealings with your fellow men. I mean that you will not need to deal with them unfairly; you do not have to get something for nothing, *but can give to every man more than you take from him.* You cannot give every man more in cash market value than you take from him, but you can give him more in use value than the cash value of the thing you take from him. The paper, ink, and other material in this book may not be worth the money you pay for it; but if the ideas suggested by it bring you thousands of dollars, you have not been wronged by those who sold it to you; they have given you a great use value for a small cash value.

Let us suppose that I own a picture by one of the great artists, which, in any civilized community, is worth thousands of dollars. I take it to Baffin Bay, and by "salesmanship" induce an Eskimo to give a bundle of furs worth $500 for it. I have really wronged him, for he has no use for the picture; it has no use value to him; it will not *add to his life.*

But suppose I give him a gun worth $50 for his furs; then he has made a good bargain. He has use for the gun; it will get him many more furs and much food; it will add to his life in every way; it will make him rich.

When you rise from the competitive to the creative plane, you can scan your business transactions very strictly, and if you are selling any man anything which does not add more to his life than the thing he give you in exchange, you can afford to stop it. You do not have to beat anybody in business. And if you are in a business which does beat people, get out of it at once.

Give every man more in use value than you take from him in cash value; then you are adding to the life of the world by every business transaction.

If you have people working for you, you must take from them more in cash value than you pay them in wages; but you can so organize your business that it will be filled with the principle of advancement, and so that each employee who wishes to do so may advance a little every day.

You can make your business do for your employees what this book is doing for you. You can so conduct your business that it will be a sort of ladder, by which every employee who will take the trouble may climb to riches himself; and given the opportunity, if he will not do so it is not your fault.

And finally, because you are to cause the creation of your riches from Formless Substance which permeates all your environment, it does not follow that they are to take shape from the atmosphere and come into being before your eyes.

If you want a sewing machine, for instance, I do not mean to tell you that you are to impress the thought of a sewing machine on Thinking Substance until the machine is formed without hands, in the room where you sit, or elsewhere. But if you want a sewing machine, hold the mental image of it with the most positive certainty that it is being made, or is on its way to you. After once forming the thought, have the most absolute and unquestioning faith that the sewing machine is coming; never think of it, or speak, of it, in any other way than as being sure to arrive. Claim it as already yours.

It will be brought to you by the power of the Supreme Intelligence, acting upon the minds of men. If you live in Maine, it may be that a man will be brought from Texas or Japan to engage in some transaction which will result in your getting what you want.

If so, the whole matter will be as much to that man's advantage as it is to yours.

Do not forget for a moment that the Thinking Substance is through all, in all, communicating with all, and can influence all. The desire of Thinking Substance for fuller life and better living has caused the creation of all the sewing machines already made; and it can cause the creation of millions more, and will, whenever men set it in motion by desire and faith, and by acting in a Certain Way.

You can certainly have a sewing machine in your house; and it is just as certain that you can have any other thing or things which you want, and which you will use for the advancement of your own life and the lives of others.

You need not hesitate about asking largely; "it is your Father's pleasure to give you the kingdom," said Jesus.

Original Substance wants to live all that is possible in you, and wants you to have all that you can or will use for the living of the most abundant life.

If you fix upon your consciousness the fact that the desire you feel for the possession of riches is one with the desire of Omnipotence for more complete expression, your faith becomes invincible.

Once I saw a little boy sitting at a piano, and vainly trying to bring harmony out of the keys; and I saw that he was grieved and provoked by his inability to play real music. I asked him the cause of his vexation, and he answered, "I can feel the music in me, but I can't make my hands go right." The music in him was the URGE of Original Substance, containing all the possibilities of all life; all that there is of music was seeking expression through the child.

God, the One Substance, is trying to live and do and enjoy things through humanity. He is saying "I want hands to build wonderful structures, to play divine harmonies, to paint glorious pictures; I want feet to run my errands, eyes to see my beauties, tongues to tell mighty truths and to sing marvelous songs," and so on.

All that there is of possibility is seeking expression through men. God wants those who can play music to have pianos and every other instrument, and to have the means to cultivate their talents to the fullest extent; He wants those who can appreciate beauty to be able to surround themselves with beautiful things; He wants those who can discern truth to have every opportunity to travel and observe; He wants those who can appreciate dress to be beautifully clothed, and those who can appreciate good food to be luxuriously fed.

He wants all these things because it is Himself that enjoys and appreciates them; it is God who wants to play, and sing, and enjoy beauty, and proclaim truth and wear fine clothes, and eat good foods. "it is God that worketh in you to will and to do," said Paul.

The desire you feel for riches is the infinite, seeking to express Himself in you as He sought to find expression in the little boy at the piano.

So you need not hesitate to ask largely.

Your part is to focalize and express the desire to God.

This is a difficult point with most people; they retain something of the old idea that poverty and self-sacrifice are pleasing to God. They look upon poverty as a part of the plan, a necessity of nature. They have the idea that God has finished His work, and made all that He can make, and that the majority of men must stay poor because there is not enough to go around. They hold to so much of this erroneous thought that they feel ashamed to ask for wealth; they try not to want more than a very modest competence, just enough to make them fairly comfortable.

I recall now the case of one student who was told that he must get in mind a clear picture of the things he desired, so that the creative thought of them might be impressed on Formless Substance. He was a very poor man, living in a rented house, and having only what he earned from day to day; and he could not grasp the fact that all wealth was his. So, after thinking the matter over, he decided that he might reasonably ask for a new rug for the floor of his best room, and an anthracite coal stove to heat the house during the cold weather. Following the instructions given in this book, he obtained these things in a few months; and then it dawned upon him that he had not asked enough. He went through the house in which he lived, and planned all the improvements he would like to make in it; he mentally added a bay window here and a room there, until it was complete in his mind as his ideal home; and then he planned its furnishings.

Holding the whole picture in his mind, he began living in the Certain Way, and moving toward what he wanted; and he owns the house now, and is rebuilding it after the form of his mental image. And now, with still larger faith, he is going on to get greater things. It has been unto him according to his faith, and it is so with you and with all of us.

Chapter 7: Gratitude

The illustrations given in the last chapter will have conveyed to the reader the fact that the first step toward getting rich is to convey the idea of your wants to the Formless Substance.

This is true, and you will see that in order to do so it becomes necessary to relate yourself to the Formless Intelligence in a harmonious way.

To secure this harmonious relation is a matter of such primary and vital importance that I shall give some space to its discussion here, and give you instructions which, if you will follow them, will be certain to bring you into perfect unity of mind with God.

The whole process of mental adjustment and atonement can be summed up in one word, gratitude.

First, you believe that there is one Intelligent Substance, from which all things proceed; second, you believe that this Substance gives you everything you desire; and third, you relate yourself to it by a feeling of deep and profound gratitude.

Many people who order their lives rightly in all other ways are kept in poverty by their lack of gratitude. Having received one gift from God, they cut the wires which connect them with Him by failing to make acknowledgment.

It is easy to understand that the nearer we live to the source of wealth, the more wealth we shall receive; and it is easy also to understand that the soul that is always grateful lives in closer touch with God than the one which never looks to Him in thankful acknowledgment.

The more gratefully we fix our minds on the Supreme when good things come to us, the more good things we will receive, and the more rapidly they will come; and the reason simply is that the mental attitude of gratitude draws the mind into closer touch with the source from which the blessings come.

If it is a new thought to you that gratitude brings your whole mind into closer harmony with the creative energies of the universe, consider it well, and you will see that it is true. The good things you already have have come to you along the line of obedience to certain laws. Gratitude will lead your mind out along the ways by which things come; and it will keep you in close harmony with creative thought and prevent you from falling into competitive thought.

Gratitude alone can keep you looking toward the All, and prevent you from falling into the error of thinking of the supply as limited; and to do that would be fatal to your hopes.

There is a Law of Gratitude, and it is absolutely necessary that you should observe the law, if you are to get the results you seek.

The law of gratitude is the natural principle that action and reaction are always equal, and in opposite directions.

The grateful outreaching of your mind in thankful praise to the Supreme *is a liberation or expenditure of force; it cannot fail to reach that to which it addressed, and the reaction is an instantaneous movement towards you.*

"Draw nigh unto God, and He will draw nigh unto you." That is a statement of psychological truth.

And if your gratitude is strong and constant, the reaction in Formless Substance will be strong and continuous; the movement of the things you want will be always toward you. Notice the grateful attitude that Jesus took; how He always seems to be saying, "I thank Thee, Father, that Thou hearest me." You cannot exercise much power without gratitude; for it is gratitude that keeps you connected with Power.

But the value of gratitude does not consist solely in getting you more blessings in the future. Without gratitude you cannot long keep from dissatisfied thought regarding things as they are.

The moment you permit your mind to dwell with dissatisfaction upon things as they are, you begin to lose ground. You fix attention upon the common, the ordinary, the poor, and the squalid and mean; and your mind takes the form of these things. Then you will transmit these forms or mental images to the Formless, and the common, the poor, the squalid, and mean will come to you.

To permit your mind to dwell upon the inferior is to become inferior and to surround yourself with inferior things.

On the other hand, to fix your attention on the best is to surround yourself with the best, and to become the best.

The Creative Power within us makes us into the image of that to which we give our attention. We are Thinking Substance, and thinking substance always takes the form of that which it thinks about.

The grateful mind is constantly fixed upon the best; therefore it tends to become the best; it takes the form or character of the best, and will receive the best.

Also, faith is born of gratitude. The grateful mind continually expects good things, and expectation becomes faith. The reaction of gratitude upon one's own mind produces faith; and every outgoing wave of grateful thanksgiving increases faith. He who has no feeling of gratitude cannot long retain a living faith; and without a living faith you cannot get rich by the creative method, as we shall see in the following chapters.

It is necessary, then, to cultivate the habit of being grateful for every good thing that comes to you; and to give thanks continuously.

And because all things have contributed to your advancement, you should include all things in your gratitude.

Do not waste time thinking or talking about the shortcomings or wrong actions of plutocrats or trust magnates. Their organization of the world has made your opportunity; all you get really comes to you because of them.

Do not rage against corrupt politicians; if it were not for politicians we should fall into anarchy, and your opportunity would be greatly lessened.

God has worked a long time and very patiently to bring us up to where we are in industry and government, and He is going right on with His work. There is not the least doubt that He will do away with plutocrats, trust magnates, captains of industry, and politicians as soon as they can be spared; but in the meantime, behold they are all very good. Remember that they are all helping to arrange the lines of transmission along which your riches will come to you, and be grateful to them all. This will bring you into harmonious relations with the good in everything, and the good in everything will move toward you.

Chapter 8: Thinking in the Certain Way

Turn back to chapter 6 and read again the story of the man who formed a mental image of his house, and you will get a fair idea of the initial step toward getting rich. You must form a clear and definite mental picture of what you want; you cannot transmit an idea unless you have it yourself.

You must have it before you can give it; and many people fail to impress Thinking Substance because they have themselves only a vague and misty concept of the things they want to do, to have, or to become.

It is not enough that you should have a general desire for wealth "to do good with"; everybody has that desire.

It is not enough that you should have a wish to travel, see things, live more, etc. Everybody has those desires also. If you were going to send a wireless message to a friend, you would not send the letters of the alphabet in their order, and let him construct the message for himself; nor would you take words at random from the dictionary. You would send a coherent sentence; one which meant something. When you try to impress your wants upon Substance, remember that it must be done by a coherent statement; you must know what you want, and be definite. You can never get rich, or start the creative power into action, by sending out unformed longings and vague desires.

Go over your desires just as the man I have described went over his house; see just what you want, and get a clear mental picture of it as you wish it to look when you get it.

That clear mental picture you must have continually in mind, as the sailor has in mind the port toward which he is sailing the ship; you must keep your face toward it all the time. You must no more lose sight of it than the steersman loses sight of the compass.

It is not necessary to take exercises in concentration, nor to set apart special times for prayer and affirmation, nor to "go into the silence," nor to do occult stunts of any kind. There things are well enough, but all you need is to know what you want, and to want it badly enough so that it will stay in your thoughts.

Spend as much of your leisure time as you can in contemplating your picture, but no one needs to take exercises to concentrate his mind on a thing which he really wants; it is the things you do not really care about which require effort to fix your attention upon them.

And unless you really want to get rich, so that the desire is strong enough to hold your thoughts directed to the purpose as the magnetic pole holds the needle of the compass, it will hardly be worth while for you to try to carry out the instructions given in this book.

The methods herein set forth are for people whose desire for riches is strong enough to overcome mental laziness and the love of ease, and make them work.

The more clear and definite you make your picture then, and the more you dwell upon it, bringing out all its delightful details, the stronger your desire will be; and the stronger your desire, the easier it will be to hold your mind fixed upon the picture of what you want.

Something more is necessary, however, than merely to see the picture clearly. If that is all you do, you are only a dreamer, and will have little or no power for accomplishment.

Behind your clear vision must be the purpose to realize it; to bring it out in tangible expression.

And behind this purpose must be an invincible and unwavering FAITH that the thing is already yours; that it is "at hand" and you have only to take possession of it.

Live in the new house, mentally, until it takes form around you physically. In the mental realm, enter at once into full enjoyment of the things you want.

"Whatsoever things ye ask for when ye pray, believe that ye receive them, and ye shall have them," said Jesus.

See the things you want as if they were actually around you all the time; see yourself as owning and using them. Make use of them in imagination just as you will use them when they are your tangible possessions. Dwell upon your mental picture until it is clear and distinct, and then take the Mental Attitude of Ownership toward everything in that picture. Take possession of it, in mind, in the full faith that it is actually yours. Hold to this mental ownership; do not waiver for an instant in the faith that it is real.

And remember what was said in a proceeding chapter about gratitude; be as thankful for it all the time as you expect to be when it has taken form. The man who can sincerely thank God for the things which as yet he owns only in imagination, has real faith. He will get rich; he will cause the creation of whatsoever he wants.

You do not need to pray repeatedly for things you want; it is not necessary to tell God about it every day.

"Use not vain repetitions as the heathen do," said Jesus said to his pupils, "for your Father knoweth the ye have need of these things before ye ask Him."

Your part is to intelligently formulate your desire for the things which make for a larger life, and to get these desire arranged into a coherent whole; and then to impress this Whole Desire upon the Formless Substance, which has the power and the will to bring you what you want.

You do not make this impression by repeating strings of words; you make it by holding the vision with unshakable PURPOSE to attain it, and with steadfast FAITH that you do attain it.

The answer to prayer is not according to your faith while you are talking, but according to your faith while you are working.

You cannot impress the mind of God by having a special Sabbath day set apart to tell Him what you want, and the forgetting Him during the rest of the week. You cannot impress Him by having special hours to go into your closet and pray, if you then dismiss the matter from your mind until the hour of prayer comes again.

Oral prayer is well enough, and has its effect, especially upon yourself, in clarifying your vision and strengthening your faith; but it is not your oral petitions which get you what you want. In order to get rich you do not need a "sweet hour of prayer"; you need to "pray without ceasing." And by prayer I mean holding steadily to your vision, with the purpose to cause its creation into solid form, and the faith that you are doing so.

"Believe that ye receive them."

The whole matter turns on receiving, once you have clearly formed your vision. When you have formed it, it is well to make an oral statement, addressing the Supreme in reverent prayer; and from that moment you must, in mind, receive what you ask for. Live in the new house; wear the fine clothes; ride in the automobile; go on the journey, and confidently plan for greater journeys. Think and speak of all the things you have asked for in terms of actual present ownership. Imagine an environment, and a financial condition exactly as you want them, and live all the time in that imaginary environment and financial condition. Mind, however, that you do not do this as a mere dreamer and castle builder; hold to the FAITH that the imaginary is being realized, and to the PURPOSE to realize it. Remember that it is faith and purpose in the use of the imagination which make the difference between the scientist and the dreamer. And having learned this fact, it is here that you must learn the proper use of the Will.

Chapter 9: How to Use the Will

To set about getting rich in a scientific way, you do not try to apply your will power to anything outside of yourself.

You have no right to do so, anyway.

It is wrong to apply your will to other men and women, in order to get them to do what you wish done.

It is as flagrantly wrong to coerce people by mental power as it is to coerce them by physical power. If compelling people by physical force to do things for you reduces them to slavery, compelling them by mental means accomplishes exactly the same thing; the only difference is in methods. If taking things from people by physical force is robbery, then taking things by mental force is robbery also; there is no difference in principle.

You have no right to use your will power upon another person, even "for his own good"; for you do not know what is for his good. The science of getting rich does not require you to apply power or force to any other person, in any way whatsoever. There is not the slightest necessity for doing so; indeed, any attempt to use your will upon others will only tend to defeat your purpose.

You do not need to apply your will to things, in order to compel them to come to you.

That would simply be trying to coerce God, and would be foolish and useless, as well as irreverent.

You do not have to compel God to give you good things, any more than you have to use your will power to make the sun rise.

You do not have to use your will power to conquer an unfriendly deity, or to make stubborn and rebellious forces do your bidding.

Substance is friendly to you, and is more anxious to give you what you want than you are to get it.

To get rich, you need only to use your will power upon yourself.

When you know what to think and do, then you must use your will to compel yourself to think and do the right things. That is the legitimate use of the will in getting what you want--to use it in holding yourself to the right course. Use your will to keep yourself thinking and acting in the Certain Way.

Do not try to project your will, or your thoughts, or your mind out into space, to "act" on things or people.

Keep your mind at home; it can accomplish more there than elsewhere.

Use your mind to form a mental image of what you want, and to hold that vision with faith and purpose; and use your will to keep your mind working in the Right Way.

The more steady and continuous your faith and purpose, the more rapidly you will get rich, because you will make only POSITIVE impressions upon Substance; and you will not neutralize or offset them by negative impressions.

The picture of your desires, held with faith and purpose, is taken up by the Formless, and permeates it to great distances-throughout the universe, for all I know.

As this impression spreads, all things are set moving toward its realization; every living thing, every inanimate thing, and the things yet uncreated, are stirred toward bringing into being that which you want. All force begins to be exerted in that direction; all things begin to move toward you. The minds of people, everywhere, are influenced toward doing the things necessary to the fulfilling of your desires; and they work for you, unconsciously.

But you can check all this by starting a negative impression in the Formless Substance. Doubt or unbelief is as certain to start a movement away from you as faith and purpose are to start one toward you. It is by not understanding this that most people who try to make use of "mental science" in getting rich make their failure. Every hour and moment you spend in giving heed to doubts and fears, every hour you spend in worry, every hour in which your soul is possessed by unbelief, sets a current away from you in the whole domain of intelligent Substance. All the promises are unto them that believe, and unto them only. Notice how insistent Jesus was upon this point of belief; and now you know the reason why.

Since belief is all important, it behooves you to guard your thoughts; and as your beliefs will be shaped to a very great extent by the things you observe and think about, it is important that you should command your attention.

And here the will comes into use; for it is by your will that you determine upon what things your attention shall be fixed.

If you want to become rich, you must not make a study of poverty.

Things are not brought into being by thinking about their opposites. Health is never to be attained by studying disease and thinking about disease; righteousness is not to be promoted by studying sin and thinking about sin; and no one ever got rich by studying poverty and thinking about poverty.

Medicine as a science of disease has increased disease; religion as a science of sin has promoted sin, and economics as a study of poverty will fill the world with wretchedness and want.

Do not talk about poverty; do not investigate it, or concern yourself with it. Never mind what its causes are; you have nothing to do with them.

What concerns you is the cure.

Do not spend your time in charitable work, or charity movements; all charity only tends to perpetuate the wretchedness it aims to eradicate.

I do not say that you should be hard hearted or unkind, and refuse to hear the cry of need; but you must not try to eradicate poverty in any of the conventional ways. Put poverty behind you, and put all that pertains to it behind you, and "make good."

Get rich; that is the best way you can help the poor.

And you cannot hold the mental image which is to make you rich if you fill your mind with pictures of poverty. Do not read books or papers which give circumstantial accounts of the wretchedness of the tenement dwellers, of the horrors of child labor, and so on. Do not read anything which fills your mind with gloomy images of want and suffering.

You cannot help the poor in the least by knowing about these things; and the wide-spread knowledge of them does not tend at all to do away with poverty.

What tends to do away with poverty is not the getting of pictures of poverty into your mind, but getting pictures of wealth into the minds of the poor.

You are not deserting the poor in their misery when you refuse to allow your mind to be filled with pictures of that misery.

Poverty can be done away with, not by increasing the number of well to do people who think about poverty, but by increasing the number of poor people who purpose with faith to get rich.

The poor do not need charity; they need inspiration. Charity only sends them a loaf of bread to keep them alive in their wretchedness, or gives them an entertainment to make them forget for an hour or two; but inspiration will cause them to rise out of their misery. If you want to help the poor, demonstrate to them that they can become rich; prove it by getting rich yourself.

The only way in which poverty will ever be banished from this world is by getting a large and constantly increasing number of people to practice the teachings of this book.

People must be taught to become rich by creation, not by competition.

Every man who becomes rich by competition throws down behind him the ladder by which he rises, and keeps others down; but every man who gets rich by creation opens a way for thousands to follow him, and inspires them to do so.

You are not showing hardness of heart or an unfeeling disposition when you refuse to pity poverty, see poverty, read about poverty, or think or talk about it, or to listen to those who do talk about it. Use your will power to keep your mind OFF the subject of poverty, and to keep it fixed with faith and purpose ON the vision of what you want.

Chapter 10: Further Use of the Will

You cannot retain a true and clear vision of wealth if you are constantly turning your attention to opposing pictures, whether they be external or imaginary.

Do not tell of your past troubles of a financial nature, if you have had them, do not think of them at all. Do not tell of the poverty of your parents, or the hardships of your early life; to do any of these things is to mentally class yourself with the poor for the time being, and it will certainly check the movement of things in your direction.

"Let the dead bury their dead," as Jesus said.

Put poverty and all things that pertain to poverty completely behind you.

You have accepted a certain theory of the universe as being correct, and are resting all your hopes of happiness on its being correct; and what can you gain by giving heed to conflicting theories?

Do not read religious books which tell you that the world is soon coming to an end; and do not read the writing of muck-rakers and pessimistic philosophers who tell you that it is going to the devil.

The world is not going to the devil; it is going to God.

It is wonderful Becoming.

True, there may be a good many things in existing conditions which are disagreeable; but what is the use of studying them when they are certainly passing away, and when the study of them only tends to check their passing and keep them with us? Why give time and attention to things which are being removed by evolutionary growth, when you can hasten their removal only by promoting the evolutionary growth as far as your part of it goes?

No matter how horrible in seeming may be the conditions in certain countries, sections, or places, you waste your time and destroy your own chances by considering them.

You should interest yourself in the world's becoming rich.

Think of the riches the world is coming into, instead of the poverty it is growing out of; and bear in mind that the only way in which you can assist the world in growing rich is by growing rich yourself through the creative method--not the competitive one.

Give your attention wholly to riches; ignore poverty.

Whenever you think or speak of those who are poor, think and speak of them as those who are becoming rich;as those who are to be congratulated rather than pitied. Then they and others will catch the inspiration, and begin to search for the way out.

Because I say that you are to give your whole time and mind and thought to riches, it does not follow that you are to be sordid or mean.

To become really rich is the noblest aim you can have in life, for it includes everything else. On the competitive plane, the struggle to get rich is a Godless scramble for power over other men; but when we come into the creative mind, all this is changed.

All that is possible in the way of greatness and soul unfoldment, of service and lofty endeavor, comes by way of getting rich; all is made possible by the use of things.

If you lack for physical health, you will find that the attainment of it is conditional on your getting rich.

Only those who are emancipated from financial worry, and who have the means to live a care-free existence and follow hygienic practices, can have and retain health.

Moral and spiritual greatness is possible only to those who are above the competitive battle for existence; and only those who are becoming rich on the plane of creative thought are free from the degrading influences of competition. If your heart is set on domestic happiness, remember that love flourishes best where there is refinement, a high level of thought, and freedom from corrupting influences; and these are to be found only where riches are attained by the exercise of creative thought, without strife or rivalry.

You can aim at nothing so great or noble, I repeat, as to become rich; and you must fix your attention upon your mental picture of riches, to the exclusion of all that may tend to dim or obscure the vision.

You must learn to see the underlying TRUTH in all things; you must see beneath all seemingly wrong conditions the Great One Life ever moving forward toward fuller expression and more complete happiness.

It is the truth that there is no such thing as poverty; that there is only wealth.

Some people remain in poverty because they are ignorant of the fact that there is wealth for them; and these can best be taught by showing them the way to affluence in your own person and practice.

Others are poor because, while they feel that there is a way out, they are too intellectually indolent to put forth the mental effort necessary to find that way and by travel it; and for these the very best thing you can do is to arouse their desire by showing them the happiness that comes from being rightly rich.

Others still are poor because, while they have some notion of science, they have become so swamped and lost in the maze of metaphysical and occult theories that they do not know which road to take. They try a mixture of many systems and fail in all. For these, again, the very best thing, to do is to show the right way in your own person and practice; an ounce of doing things is worth a pound of theorizing.

The very best thing you can do for the whole world is to make the most of yourself.

You can serve God and man in no more effective way than by getting rich; that is, if you get rich by the creative method and not by the competitive one.

Another thing. We assert that this book gives in detail the principles of the science of getting rich; and if that is true, you do not need to read any other book upon the subject. This may sound narrow and egotistical, but consider: there is no more scientific method of computation in mathematics than by addition, subtraction, multiplication, and division; no other method is possible. There can be but one shortest distance between two points. There is only one way to think scientifically, and that is to think in the way that leads by the most direct and simple route to the goal. No man has yet formulated a briefer or less complex "system" than the one set forth herein; it has been stripped of all non-essentials. When you commence on this, lay all others aside; put them out of your mind altogether.

Read this book every day; keep it with you; commit it to memory, and do not think about other "systems" and theories. If you do, you will begin to have doubts, and to be uncertain and wavering in your thought; and then you will begin to make failures.

After you have made good and become rich, you may study other systems as much as you please; but until you are quite sure that you have gained what you want, do not read anything on this line but this book, unless it be the authors mentioned in the Preface.

And read only the most optimistic comments on the world's news; those in harmony with your picture.

Also, postpone your investigations into the occult. Do not dabble in theosophy, Spiritualism, or kindred studies. It is very likely that the dead still live, and are near; but if they are, let them alone; mind your own business.

Wherever the spirits of the dead may be, they have their own work to do, and their own problems to solve; and we have no right to interfere with them. We cannot help them, and it is very doubtful whether they can help us, or whether we have any right to trespass upon their time if they can. Let the dead and the hereafter alone, and solve your own problem; get rich. If you begin to mix with the occult, you will start mental cross-currents which will surely bring your hopes to shipwreck. Now, this and the preceding chapters have brought us to the following statement of basic facts:–

There is a thinking stuff from which all things are made, and which, in its original state, permeates, penetrates, and fills the interspaces of the universe.

A thought, in this substance, Produces the thing that is imaged by the thought.

Man can form things in his thought, and, by impressing his thought upon formless substance, can cause the thing he thinks about to be created.

In order to do this, man must pass from the competitive to the creative mind; he must form a clear mental picture of the things he wants, and hold this picture in his thoughts with the fixed PURPOSE to get what he wants, and the unwavering FAITH that he does get what he wants, closing his mind against all that may tend to shake his purpose, dim his vision, or quench his faith.

And in addition to all this, we shall now see that he must live and act in a Certain Way.

Chapter 11: Acting in the Certain Way

Thought is the creative power, or the impelling force which causes the creative power to act; thinking in a Certain Way will bring riches to you, but you must not rely upon thought alone, paying no attention to personal action. That is the rock upon which many otherwise scientific metaphysical thinkers meet shipwreck--the failure to connect thought with personal action.

We have not yet reached the stage of development, even supposing such a stage to be possible, in which man can create directly from Formless Substance without nature's processes or the work of human hands; man must not only think, but his personal action must supplement his thought.

By thought you can cause the gold in the hearts of the mountains to be impelled toward you; but it will not mine itself, refine itself, coin itself into double eagles, and come rolling along the roads seeking its way into your pocket.

Under the impelling power of the Supreme Spirit, men's affairs will be so ordered that some one will be led to mine the gold for you; other men's business transactions will be so directed that the gold will be brought toward you, and you must so arrange your own business affairs that you may be able to receive it when it comes to you. Your thought makes all things, animate and inanimate, work to bring you what you want; but your personal activity must be such that you can rightly receive what you want when it reaches you. You are not to take it as charity, nor to steal it; you must give every man more in use value than he gives you in cash value.

The scientific use of thought consists in forming a clear and distinct mental image of what you want; in holding fast to the purpose to get what you want; and in realizing with grateful faith that you do get what you want.

Do not try to 'project' your thought in any mysterious or occult way, with the idea of having it go out and do things for you; that is wasted effort, and will weaken your power to think with sanity.

The action of thought in getting rich is fully explained in the preceding chapters; your faith and purpose positively impress your vision upon Formless Substance, which has THE SAME DESIRE FOR MORE LIFE THAT YOU HAVE; and this vision, received from you, sets all the creative forces at work IN AND THROUGH THEIR REGULAR CHANNELS OF ACTION, but directed toward you.

It is not your part to guide or supervise the creative process; all you have to do with that is to retain your vision, stick to your purpose, and maintain your faith and gratitude.

But you must act in a Certain Way, so that you can appropriate what is yours when it comes to you; so that you can meet the things you have in your picture, and put them in their proper places as they arrive.

You can really see the truth of this. When things reach you, they will be in the hands of other men, who will ask an equivalent for them.

And you can only get what is yours by giving the other man what is his.

Your pocketbook is not going to be transformed into a Fortunata's purse, which shall be always full of money without effort on your part.

This is the crucial point in the science of getting rich; right here, where thought and personal action must be combined. There are very many people who, consciously or unconsciously, set the creative forces in action by the strength and persistence of their desires, but who remain poor because they do not provide for the reception of the thing they want when it comes.

By thought, the thing you want is brought to you; by action you receive it.

Whatever your action is to be, it is evident that you must act NOW. You cannot act in the past, and it is essential to the clearness of your mental vision that you dismiss the past from your mind. You cannot act in the future, for the future is not here yet. And you cannot tell how you will want to act in any future contingency until that contingency has arrived.

Because you are not in the right business, or the right environment now, do not think that you must postpone action until you get into the right business or environment. And do not spend time in the present taking thought as to the best course in possible future emergencies; have faith in your ability to meet any emergency when it arrives.

If you act in the present with your mind on the future, your present action will be with a divided mind, and will not be effective.

Put your whole mind into present action.

Do not give your creative impulse to Original Substance, and then sit down and wait for results; if you do, you will never get them. Act now. There is never any time but now, and there never will be any time but now. If you are ever to begin to make ready for the reception of what you want, you must begin now.

And your action, whatever it is, must most likely be in your present business or employment, and must be upon the persons and things in your present environment.

You cannot act where you are not; you cannot act where you have been, and you cannot act where you are going to be; you can act only where you are.

Do not bother as to whether yesterday's work was well done or ill done; do to-day's work well. Do not try to do tomorrow's work now; there will be plenty of time to do that when you get to it.

Do not try, by occult or mystical means, to act on people or things that are out of your reach.

Do not wait for a change of environment, before you act; get a change of environment by action.

You can so act upon the environment in which you are now, as to cause yourself to be transferred to a better environment.

Hold with faith and purpose the vision of yourself in the better environment, but act upon your present environment with all your heart, and with all your strength, and with all your mind.

Do not spend any time in day dreaming or castle building; hold to the one vision of what you want, and act NOW.

Do not cast about seeking some new thing to do, or some strange, unusual, or remarkable action to perform as a first step toward getting rich. It is probable that your actions, at least for some time to come, will be those you have been performing for some time past; but you are to begin now to perform these actions in the Certain Way, which will surely make you rich.

If you are engaged in some business, and feel that it is not the right one for you, do not wait until you get into the right business before you begin to act.

Do not feel discouraged, or sit down and lament because you are misplaced. No man was ever so misplaced but that he could not find the right place, and no man ever became so involved in the wrong business but that he could get into the right business.

Hold the vision of yourself in the right business, with the purpose to get into it, and the faith that you will get into it, and are getting into it; but ACT in your present business. Use your present business as the means of getting a better one, and use your present enviornment as the means of getting into a better one. Your vision of the right business, if held with faith and purpose, will cause the Supreme to move the right business toward you; and your action, if performed in the Certain Way, will cause you to move toward the business.

If you are an employee, or wage earner, and feel that you must change places in order to get what you want, do not 'project" your thought into space and rely upon it to get you another job. It will probably fail to do so.

Hold the vision of yourself in the job you want, while you ACT with faith and purpose on the job you have, and you will certainly get the job you want.

Your vision and faith will set the creative force in motion to bring it toward you, and your action will cause the forces in your own environment to move you toward the place you want. In closing this chapter, we will add another statement to our syllabus:–

There is a thinking stuff from which all things are made, and which, in its original state, permeates, penetrates, and fills the interspaces of the universe.

A thought, in this substance, Produces the thing that is imaged by the thought.

Man can form things in his thought, and, by impressing his thought upon formless substance, can cause the thing he thinks about to be created.

In order to do this, man must pass from the competitive to the creative mind; he must form a clear mental picture of the things he wants, and hold this picture in his thoughts with the fixed PURPOSE to get what he wants, and the unwavering FAITH that he does get what he wants, closing his mind to all that may tend to shake his purpose, dim his vision, or quench his faith.

That he may receive what he wants when it comes, man must act NOW upon the people and things in his present environment.

Chapter 12: Efficient Action

You must use your thought as directed in previous chapters, and begin to do what you can do where you are; and you must do ALL that you can do where you are.

You can advance only by being larger than your present place; and no man is larger than his present place who leaves undone any of the work pertaining to that place.

The world is advanced only by those who more than fill their present places.

If no man quite filled his present place, you can see that there must be a going backward in everything. Those who do not quite fill their present places are dead weight upon society, government, commerce, and industry; they must be carried along by others at a great expense. The progress of the world is retarded only by those who do not fill the places they are holding; they belong to a former age and a lower stage or plane of life, and their tendency is toward degeneration. No society could advance if every man was smaller than his place; social evolution is guided by the law of physical and mental evolution. In the animal world, evolution is caused by excess of life.

When an organism has more life than can be expressed in the functions of its own plane, it develops the organs of a higher plane, and a new species is originated.

There never would have been new species had there not been organisms which more than filled their places. The law is exactly the same for you; your getting rich depends upon your applying this principle to your own affairs.

Every day is either a successful day or a day of failure; and it is the successful days which get you what you want. If everyday is a failure, you can never get rich; while if every day is a success, you cannot fail to get rich.

If there is something that may be done today, and you do not do it, you have failed in so far as that thing is concerned; and the consequences may be more disastrous than you imagine.

You cannot foresee the results of even the most trivial act; you do not know the workings of all the forces that have been set moving in your behalf. Much may be depending on your doing some simple act; it may be the very thing which is to open the door of opportunity to very great possibilities. You can never know all the combinations which Supreme Intelligence is making for you in the world of things and of things and of human affairs; your neglect or failure to do some small thing may cause a long delay in getting what you want.

Do, every day, ALL that can be done that day.

There is, however, a limitation or qualification of the above that you must take into account.

You are not to overwork, nor to rush blindly into your business in the effort to do the greatest possible number of things in the shortest possible time.

You are not to try to do tomorrow's work today, nor to do a week's work in a day.

It is really not the number of things you do, but the EFFICIENCY of each separate action that counts.

Every act is, in itself, either a success or a failure.

Every act is, in itself, either effective or inefficient.

Every inefficient act is a failure, and if you spend your life in doing inefficient acts, your whole life will be a failure.

The more things you do, the worse for you, if all your acts are inefficient ones.

On the other hand, every efficient act is a success in itself, and if every act of your life is an efficient one, your whole life MUST be a success.

The cause of failure is doing too many things in an inefficient manner, and not doing enough things in an efficient manner.

You will see that it is a self-evident proposition that if you do not do any inefficient acts, and if you do a sufficient number of efficient acts, you will become rich. If, now, it is possible for you to make each act an efficient one, you see again that the getting of riches is reduced to an exact science, like mathematics.

The matter turns, then, on the questions whether you can make each separate act a success in itself. And this you can certainly do.

You can make each act a success, because ALL Power is working with you; and ALL Power cannot fail.

Power is at your service; and to make each act efficient you have only to put power into it.

Every action is either strong or weak; and when every one is strong, you are acting in the Certain Way which will make you rich.

Every act can be made strong and efficient by holding your vision while you are doing it, and putting the whole power of your FAITH and PURPOSE into it.

It is at this point that the people fail who separate mental power from personal action. They use the power of mind in one place and at one time, and they act in another place and at another time. So their acts are not successful in themselves; too many of them are inefficient. But if ALL Power goes into every act, no matter how commonplace, every act will be a success in itself; and as in the nature of things every success opens the way to other successes, your progress toward what you want, and the progress of what you want toward you, will become increasingly rapid.

Remember that successful action is cumulative in its results. Since the desire for more life is inherent in all things, when a man begins to move toward larger life more things attach themselves to him, and the influence of his desire is multiplied.

Do, every day, all that you can do that day, and do each act in an efficient manner.

In saying that you must hold your vision while you are doing each act, however trivial or commonplace, I do not mean to say that it is necessary at all times to see the vision distinctly to its smallest details. It should be the work of your leisure hours to use your imagination on the details of your vision, and to contemplate them until they are firmly fixed upon memory. If you wish speedy results, spend practically all your spare time in this practice.

By continuous contemplation you will get the picture of what you want, even to the smallest details, so firmly fixed upon your mind, and so completely transferred to the mind of Formless Substance, that in your working hours you need only to mentally refer to the picture to stimulate your faith and purpose, and cause your best effort to be put forth. Contemplate your picture in your leisure hours until your consciousness is so full of it that you can grasp it instantly. You will become so enthused with its bright promises that the mere thought of it will call forth the strongest energies of your whole being.

Let us again repeat our syllabus, and by slightly changing the closing statements bring it to the point we have now reached.

There is a thinking stuff from which all things are made, and which, in its original state, permeates, penetrates, and fills the interspaces of the universe.

A thought, in this substance, Produces the thing that is imaged by the thought.

Man can form things in his thought, and, by impressing his thought upon formless substance, can cause the thing he thinks about to be created.

In order to do this, man must pass from the competitive to the creative mind; he must form a clear mental picture of the things he wants, and do, with faith and purpose, all that can be done each day, doing each separate thing in an efficient manner.

Chapter 13: Getting into the Right Business

Success, in any particular business, depends for one thing upon your possessing in a well-developed state the faculties required in that business.

Without good musical faculty no one can succeed as a teacher of music; without well-developed mechanical faculties no one can achieve great success in any of the mechanical trades; without tact and the commercial faculties no one can succeed in mercantile pursuits. But to possess in a well-developed state the faculties required in your particular vocation does not insure getting rich. There are musicians who have remarkable talent, and who yet remain poor; there are blacksmiths, carpenters, and so on who have excellent mechanical ability, but who do not get rich; and there are merchants with good faculties for dealing with men who nevertheless fail.

The different faculties are tools; it is essential to have good tools, but it is also essential that the tools should be used in the Right Way. One man can take a sharp saw, a square, a good plane, and so on, and build a handsome article of furniture; another man can take the same tools and set to work to duplicate the article, but his production will be a botch. He does not know how to use good tools in a successful way.

The various faculties of your mind are the tools with which you must do the work which is to make you rich; it will be easier for you to succeed if you get into a business for which you are well equipped with mental tools.

Generally speaking, you will do best in that business which will use your strongest faculties; the one for which you are naturally "best fitted." But there are limitations to this statement, also.

No man should regard his vocation as being irrevocably fixed by the tendencies with which he was born.

You can get rich in ANY business, for if you have not the right talent for you can develop that talent; it merely means that you will have to make your tools as you go along, instead of confining yourself to the use of those with which you were born. It will be EASIER for you to succeed in a vocation for which you already have the talents in a well-developed state; but you CAN succeed in any vocation, for you can develop any rudimentary talent, and there is no talent of which you have not at least the rudiment.

You will get rich most easily in point of effort, if you do that for which you are best fitted; but you will get rich most satisfactorily if you do that which you WANT to do.

Doing what you want to do is life; and there is no real satisfaction in living if we are compelled to be forever doing something which we do not like to do, and can never do what we want to do. And it is certain that you can do what you want to do; the desire to do it is proof that you have within you the power which *can* do it.

Desire is a manifestation of power.

The desire to play music is the power which can play music seeking expression and development; the desire to invent mechanical devices is the mechanical talent seeking expression and development.

Where there is no power, either developed or undeveloped, to do a thing, there is never any desire to do that thing; and where there is strong desire to do a thing, it is certain proof that the power to do it is strong, and only requires to be developed and applied in the Right Way.

All things else being equal, it is best to select the business for which you have the best developed talent; but if you have a strong desire to engage in any particular line of work, you should select that work as the ultimate end at which you aim.

You can do what you want to do, and it is your right and privilege to follow the business or avocation which will be most congenial and pleasant.

You are not obliged to do what you do not like to do, and should not do it except as a means to bring you to the doing of the thing you want to do.

If there are past mistakes whose consequences have placed you in an undesirable business or environment, you may be obliged for some time to do what you do not like to do; but you can make the doing of it pleasant by knowing that it is making it possible for you to come to the doing of what you want to do.

If you feel that you are not in the right vocation, do not act too hastily in trying to get into another one. The best way, generally, to change business or environment is by growth.

Do not be afraid to make a sudden and radical change if the opportunity is presented, and you feel after careful consideration that it is the right opportunity; but never take sudden or radical action when you are in doubt as to the wisdom of doing so.

There is never any hurry on the creative plane; and there is no lack of opportunity.

When you get out of the competitive mind you will understand that you never need to act hastily. No one else is going to beat you to the thing you want to do; there is enough for all. If one space is taken, another and a better one will be opened for you a little farther on; there is plenty of time. When you are in doubt, wait. Fall back on the contemplation of your vision, and increase your faith and purpose; and by all means, in times of doubt and indecision, cultivate gratitude.

A day or two spent in contemplating the vision of what you want, and in earnest thanksgiving that you are getting it, will bring your mind into such close relationship with the Supreme that you will make no mistake when you do act.

There is a mind which knows all there is to know; and you can come into close unity with this mind by faith and the purpose to advance in life, if you have deep gratitude.

Mistakes come from acting hastily, or from acting in fear or doubt, or in forgetfulness of the Right Motive, which is more life to all, and less to none.

As you go on in the Certain Way, opportunities will come to you in increasing number; and you will need to be very steady in your faith and purpose, and to keep in close touch with the All Mind by reverent gratitude.

Do all that you can do in a perfect manner every day, but do it without haste, worry, or fear. Go as fast as you can, but never hurry.

Remember that in the moment you begin to hurry you cease to be a creator and become a competitor; you drop back upon the old plane again.

Whenever you find yourself hurrying, call a halt; fix your attention on the mental image of the thing you want, and begin to give thanks that you are getting it. The exercise of GRATITUDE will never fail to strengthen your faith and renew your purpose.

Chapter 14: The Impression of Increase

Whether you change your vocation or not, your actions for the present must be those pertaining to the business in which you are now engaged.

You can get into the business you want by making constructive use of the business you are already established in; by doing your daily work in a Certain Way.

And in so far as your business consists in dealing with other men, whether personally or by letter, the key-thought of all your efforts must be to convey to their minds the impression of increase.

Increase is what all men and all women are seeking; it is the urge of the Formless Intelligence within them, seeking fuller expression.

The desire for increase is inherent in all nature; it is the fundamental impulse of the universe. All human activities are based on the desire for increase; people are seeking more food, more clothes, better shelter, more luxury, more beauty, more knowledge, more pleasure-- increase in something, more life.

Every living thing is under this necessity for continuous advancement; where increase of life ceases, dissolution and death set in at once.

Man instinctively knows this, and hence he is forever seeking more. This law of perpetual increase is set forth by Jesus in the parable of the talents; only those who gain more retain any; from him who hath not shall be taken away even that which he hath.

The normal desire for increased wealth is not an evil or a reprehensible thing; it is simply the desire for more abundant life; it is aspiration.

And because it is the deepest instinct of their natures, all men and women are attracted to him who can give them more of the means of life.

In following the Certain Way as described in the foregoing pages, you are getting continuous increase for yourself, and you are giving it to all with whom you deal.

You are a creative center, from which increase is given off to all.

Be sure of this, and convey assurance of the fact to every man, woman, and child with whom you come in contact. No matter how small the transaction, even if it be only the selling of a stick of candy to a little child, put into it the thought of increase, and make sure that the customer is impressed with the thought.

Convey the impression of advancement with everything you do, so that all people shall receive the impression that you are an Advancing Man, and that you advance all who deal with you. Even to the people whom you meet in a social way, without any thought of business, and to whom you do not try to sell anything, give the thought of increase.

You can convey this impression by holding the unshakable faith that you, yourself, are in the Way of Increase; and by letting this faith inspire, fill, and permeate every action.

Do everything that you do in the firm conviction that you are an advancing personality, and that you are giving advancement to everybody.

Feel that you are getting rich, and that in so doing you are making others rich, and conferring benefits on all.

Do not boast or brag of your success, or talk about it unnecessarily; true faith is never boastful.

Wherever you find a boastful person, you find one who is secretly doubtful and afraid. Simply feel the faith, and let it work out in every transaction; let every act and tone and look express the quiet assurance that you are getting rich; that you are already rich. Words will not be necessary to communicate this feeling to others; they will feel the sense of increase when in your presence, and will be attracted to you again.

You must so impress others that they will feel that in associating with you they will get increase for themselves. See that you give them a use value greater than the cash value you are taking from them.

Take an honest pride in doing this, and let everybody know it; and you will have no lack of customers. People will go where they are given increase; and the Supreme, which desires increase in all, and which knows all, will move toward you men and women who have never heard of you. Your business will increase rapidly, and you will be surprised at the unexpected benefits which will come to you. You will be able from day to day to make larger combinations, secure greater advantages, and to go on into a more congenial vocation if you desire to do so.

But in doing all this, you must never lose sight of your vision of what you want, or your faith and purpose to get what you want.

Let me here give you another word of caution in regard to motives.

Beware of the insidious temptation to seek for power over other men.

Nothing is so pleasant to the unformed or partially developed mind as the exercise of power or dominion over others. *The desire to rule for selfish gratification has been the curse of the world.* For countless ages kings and lords have drenched the earth with blood in their battles to extend their dominions; this not to seek more life for all, but to get more power for themselves.

Today, the main motive in the business and industrial world is the same; men marshal their armies of dollars, and lay waste the lives and hearts of millions in the same mad scramble for power over others. Commercial kings, like political kings, are inspired by the lust for power.

Jesus saw in this desire for mastery the moving impulse of that evil world He sought to overthrow. Read the twenty-third chapter of Matthew, and see how He pictures the lust of the Pharisees to be called "Master," to sit in the high places, to domineer over others, and to lay burdens on the backs of the less fortunate; and note how He compares this lust for dominion with the brotherly seeking for the Common Good to which He calls His disciples.

Look out for the temptation to seek for authority, to become a "master," to be considered as one who is above the common herd, to impress others by lavish display, and so on.

The mind that seeks for mastery over others is the competitive mind; and the competitive mind is not the creative one. In order to master your environment and your destiny, it is not at all necessary that you should rule over your fellow men and indeed, when you fall into the world's struggle for the high places, you begin to be conquered by fate and environment, and your getting rich becomes a matter of chance and speculation.

Beware of the competitive mind!! No better statement of the principle of creative action can be formulated than the favorite declaration of the late "Golden Rule" Jones of Toledo: "What I want for myself, I want for everybody."

Chapter 15: The Advancing Man

What I have said in the last chapter applies as well to the professional man and the wage-earner as to the man who is engaged in mercantile business.

No matter whether you are a physician, a teacher, or a clergyman, if you can give increase of life to others and make them sensible of the fact, they will be attracted to you, and you will get rich. The physician who holds the vision of himself as a great and successful healer, and who works toward the complete realization of that vision with faith and purpose, as described in former chapters, will come into such close touch with the Source of Life that he will be phenomenally successful; patients will come to him in throngs.

No one has a greater opportunity to carry into effect the teaching of this book than the practitioner of medicine; it does not matter to which of the various schools he may belong, for the principle of healing is common to all of them, and may be reached by all alike. The Advancing Man in medicine, who holds to a clear mental image of himself as successful, and who obeys the laws of faith, purpose, and gratitude, will cure every curable case he undertakes, no matter what remedies he may use.

In the field of religion, the world cries out for the clergyman who can teach his hearers the true science of abundant life. He who masters the details of the science of getting rich, together with the allied sciences of being well, of being great, and of winning love, and who teaches these details from the pulpit, will never lack for a congregation. This is the gospel that the world needs; it will give increase of life, and men will hear it gladly, and will give liberal support to the man who brings it to them.

What is now needed is a demonstration of the science of life from the pulpit. We want preachers who can not only tell us how, but who in their own persons will show us how. We need the preacher who will himself be rich, healthy, great, and beloved, to teach us how to attain to these things; and when he comes he will find a numerous and loyal following.

The same is true of the teacher who can inspire the children with the faith and purpose of the advancing life. He will never be "out of a job." And any teacher who has this faith and purpose can give it to his pupils; he cannot help giving it to them if it is part of his own life and practice.

What is true of the teacher, preacher, and physician is true of the lawyer, dentist, real estate man, insurance agent--of everybody.

The combined mental and personal action I have described is infallible; it cannot fail. Every man and woman who follows these instructions steadily, perseveringly, and to the letter, will get rich. The law of the Increase of Life is as mathematically certain in its operation as the law of gravitation; getting rich is an exact science.

The wage-earner will find this as true of his case as of any of the others mentioned. Do not feel that you have no chance to get rich because you are working where there is no visible opportunity for advancement, where wages are small and the cost of living high. Form your clear mental vision of what you want, and begin to act with faith and purpose.

Do all the work you can do, every day, and do each piece of work in a perfectly successful manner; put the power of success, and the purpose to get rich, into everything that you do.

But do not do this merely with the idea of currying favor with your employer, in the hope that he, or those above you, will see your good work and advance you; it is not likely that they will do so.

The man who is merely a "good" workman, filling his place to the very best of his ability, and satisfied with that, is valuable to his employer; and it is not to the employer's interest to promote him; he is worth more where he is.

To secure advancement, something more is necessary than to be too large for your place.

The man who is certain to advance is the one who is too big for his place, and who has a clear concept of what he wants to be; who knows that he can become what he wants to be and who is determined to BE what he wants to be.

Do not try to more than fill your present place with a view to pleasing your employer; do it with the idea of advancing yourself. Hold the faith and purpose of increase during work hours, after work hours, and before work hours. Hold it in such a way that every person who comes in contact with you, whether foreman, fellow workman, or social acquaintance, will feel the power of purpose radiating from you; so that every one will get the sense of advancement and increase from you. Men will be attracted to you, and if there is no possibility for advancement in your present job, you will very soon see an opportunity to take another job.

There is a Power which never fails to present opportunity to the Advancing Man who is moving in obedience to law.

God cannot help helping you, if you act in a Certain Way; He must do so in order to help Himself.

There is nothing in your circumstances or in the industrial situation that can keep you down. If you cannot get rich working for the steel trust, you can get rich on a ten-acre farm; and if you begin to move in the Certain Way, you will certainly escape from the "clutches" of the steel trust and get on to the farm or wherever else you wish to be.

If a few thousands of its employees would enter upon the Certain Way, the steel trust would soon be in a bad plight; it would have to give its workingmen more opportunity, or go out of business. Nobody has to work for a trust; the trusts can keep men in so called hopeless conditions only so long as there are men who are too ignorant to know of the science of getting rich, or too intellectually slothful to practice it.

Begin this way of thinking and acting, and your faith and purpose will make you quick to see any opportunity to better your condition.

Such opportunities will speedily come, for the Supreme, working in All, and working for you, will bring them before you.

Do not wait for an opportunity to be all that you want to be; when an opportunity to be more than you are now is presented and you feel impelled toward it, take it. It will be the first step toward a greater opportunity.

There is no such thing possible in this universe as a lack of opportunities for the man who is living the advancing life.

It is inherent in the constitution of the cosmos that all things shall be for him and work together for his good; and he must certainly get rich if he acts and thinks in the Certain Way. So let wage-earning men and women study this book with great care, and enter with confidence upon the course of action it prescribes; it will not fail.

Chapter 16: Some Cautions, and Concluding Observations

Many people will scoff at the idea that there is an exact science of getting rich; holding the impression that the supply of wealth is limited, they will insist that social and governmental institutions must be changed before even any considerable number of people can acquire a competence.

But this is not true.

It is true that existing governments keep the masses in poverty, but this is because the masses do not think and act in the Certain Way.

If the masses begin to move forward as suggested in this book, neither governments nor industrial systems can check them; all systems must be modified to accommodate the forward movement.

If the people have the Advancing Mind, have the Faith that they can become rich, and move forward with the fixed purpose to become rich, nothing can possibly keep them in poverty.

Individuals may enter upon the Certain Way at any time, and under any government, and make themselves rich; and when any considerable number of individuals do so under any government, they will cause the system to be so modified as to open the way for others.

The more men who get rich on the competitive plane, the worse for others; the more who get rich on the creative plane, the better for others.

The economic salvation of the masses can only be accomplished by getting a large number of people to practice the scientific method set down in this book, and become rich. These will show others the way, and inspire them with a desire for real life, with the faith that it can be attained, and with the purpose to attain it.

For the present, however, it is enough to know that neither the government under which you live nor the capitalistic or competitive system of industry can keep you from getting rich. When you enter upon the creative plane of thought you will rise above all these things and become a citizen of another kingdom.

But remember that your thought must be held upon the creative plane; you are never for an instant to be betrayed into regarding the supply as limited, or into acting on the moral level of competition.

Whenever you do fall into old ways of thought, correct yourself instantly; for when you are in the competitive mind, you have lost the cooperation of the Mind of the Whole.

Do not spend any time in planning as to how you will meet possible emergencies in the future, except as the necessary policies may affect your actions today. You are concerned with doing today's work in a perfectly successful manner, and not with emergencies which may arise tomorrow; you can attend to them as they come.

Do not concern yourself with questions as to how you shall surmount obstacles which may loom upon your business horizon, unless you can see plainly that your course must be altered today in order to avoid them.

No matter how tremendous an obstruction may appear at a distance, you will find that if you go on in the Certain Way it will disappear as you approach it, or that a way over, through, or around it will appear.

No possible combination of circumstances can defeat a man or woman who is proceeding to get rich along strictly scientific lines. No man or woman who obeys the law can fail to get rich, any more than one can multiply two by two and fail to get four.

Give no anxious thought to possible disasters, obstacles, panics, or unfavorable combinations of circumstances; it is time enough to meet such things when they present themselves before you in the immediate present, and you will find that every difficulty carries with it the wherewithal for its overcoming.

Guard your speech. Never speak of yourself, your affairs, or of anything else in a discouraged or discouraging way.

Never admit the possibility of failure, or speak in a way that infers failure as a possibility.

Never speak of the times as being hard, or of business conditions as being doubtful. Times may be hard and business doubtful for those who are on the competitive plane, but they can never be so for you; you can create what you want, and you are above fear.

When others are having hard times and poor business, you will find your greatest opportunities.

Train yourself to think of and to look upon the world as a something which is Becoming, which is growing; and to regard seeming evil as being only that which is undeveloped. Always speak in terms of advancement; to do otherwise is to deny your faith, and to deny your faith is to lose it.

Never allow yourself to feel disappointed. You may expect to have a certain thing at a certain time, and not get it at that time; and this will appear to you like failure.

But if you hold to your faith you will find that the failure is only apparent.

Go on in the certain way, and if you do not receive that thing, you will receive something so much better that you will see that the seeming failure was really a great success.

A student of this science had set his mind on making a certain business combination which seemed to him at the time to be very desirable, and he worked for some weeks to bring it about. When the crucial time came, the thing failed in a perfectly inexplicable way; it was as if some unseen influence had been working secretly against him. He was not disappointed; on the contrary, he thanked God that his desire had been overruled, and went steadily on with a grateful mind. In a few weeks an opportunity so much better came his way that he would not have made the first deal on any account; and he saw that a Mind which knew more than he knew had prevented him from losing the greater good by entangling himself with the lesser.

That is the way every seeming failure will work out for you, if you keep your faith, hold to your purpose, have gratitude, and do, every day, all that can be done that day, doing each separate act in a successful manner.

When you make a failure, it is because you have not asked for enough; keep on, and a larger thing then you were seeking will certainly come to you. Remember this.

You will not fail because you lack the necessary talent to do what you wish to do. If you go on as I have directed, you will develop all the talent that is necessary to the doing of your work.

It is not within the scope of this book to deal with the science of cultivating talent; but it is as certain and simple as the process of getting rich.

However, do not hesitate or waver for fear that when you come to any certain place you will fail for lack of ability; keep right on, and when you come to that place, the ability will be furnished to you. The same source of Ability which enabled the untaught Lincoln to do the greatest work in government ever accomplished by a single man is open to you; you may draw upon all the mind there is for wisdom to use in meeting the responsibilities which are laid upon you. Go on in full faith.

Study this book. Make it your constant companion until you have mastered all the ideas contained in it. While you are getting firmly established in this faith, you will do well to give up most recreations and pleasure; and to stay away from places where ideas conflicting with these are advanced in lectures or sermons. Do not read pessimistic or conflicting literature, or get into arguments upon the matter. Do very little reading, outside of the writers mentioned in the Preface. Spend most of your leisure time in contemplating your vision, and in cultivating gratitude, and in reading this book. It contains all you need to know of the science of getting rich; and you will find all the essentials summed up in the following chapter.

Chapter 17: Summary of the Science of Getting Rich

There is a thinking stuff from which all things are made, and which, in its original state, permeates, penetrates, and fills the interspaces of the universe.

A thought in this substance produces the thing that is imaged by the thought.

Man can form things in his thought, and by impressing his thought upon formless substance can cause the thing he thinks about to be created.

In order to do this, man must pass from the competitive to the creative mind; otherwise he cannot be in harmony with the Formless Intelligence, which is always creative and never competitive in spirit.

Man may come into full harmony with the Formless Substance by entertaining a lively and sincere gratitude for the blessings it bestows upon him. Gratitude unifies the mind of man with the intelligence of Substance, so that man's thoughts are received by the Formless. Man can remain upon the creative plane only by uniting himself with the Formless Intelligence through a deep and continuous feeling of gratitude.

Man must form a clear and definite mental image of the things he wishes to have, to do, or to become; and he must hold this mental image in his thoughts, while being deeply grateful to the Supreme that all his desires are granted to him. The man who wishes to get rich must spend his leisure hours in contemplating his Vision, and in earnest thanksgiving that the reality is being given to him. Too much stress cannot be laid on the importance of frequent contemplation of the mental image, coupled with unwavering faith and devout gratitude. This is the process by which the impression is given to the Formless, and the creative forces set in motion.

The creative energy works through the established channels of natural growth, and of the industrial and social order. All that is included in his mental image will surely be brought to the man who follows the instructions given above, and whose faith does not waver. What he wants will come to him through the ways of established trade and commerce.

In order to receive his own when it shall come to him, man must be active; and this activity can only consist in more than filling his present place. He must keep in mind the Purpose to get rich through the realization of his mental image. And he must do, every day, all that can be done that day, taking care to do each act in a successful manner. He must give to every man a use value in excess of the cash value he receives, so that each transaction makes for more life; and he must so hold the Advancing Thought that the impression of increase will be communicated to all with whom he comes in contact.

The men and women who practice the foregoing instructions will certainly get rich; and the riches they receive will be in exact proportion to the definiteness of their vision, the fixity of their purpose, the steadiness of their faith, and the depth of their gratitude.

www.ingramcontent.com/pod-product-compliance
Lightning Source LLC
Chambersburg PA
CBHW071439300726
48976CB00004B/1388